A TIME OF DIFFICULT TRANSITIONS: CANADA-U.S. RELATIONS IN 1976

A Staff Report

CANADIAN-AMERICAN COMMITTEE
sponsored by
C. D. Howe Research Institute (Canada)
National Planning Association (U.S.A.)

Legal Deposit — 3rd Quarter 1976
Quebec National Library
Library of Congress Catalogue Number 76-21944
ISBN 0-88806-018-1
July, 1976, $2.00

Quotation with appropriate credit is permissible

C.D. Howe Research Institute (Montreal, Quebec) and
National Planning Association (Washington, D.C.)

Printed in Canada

PREFACE

The existence of a unique and important relationship between Canada and the United States is a fact. It is in both countries' national interest to seek to maintain basic friendship and cooperation in this relationship, but that task requires patient effort in the face of contemporary economic and political strains. Too often, public perceptions of the relationship are shaped by dramatic accounts of issues arising from these strains. There is in neither country at this time a systematic process for putting these issues into a broader perspective through regular, independent reviews and commentaries that are available to the public. Recent foreign policy surveys by both governments have either neglected the bilateral relationship or treated it as a special problem area. Media reporting on the relationship tends to focus upon current policy disputes without providing continuity of analysis or a longer-term context.

Recognizing the need for prompt and continuing commentary on the bilateral relationship from a broad and informed perspective, the Canadian-American Committee has sought to expand its publication activities in the past few years. Since it was established in 1957, the Committee has published nearly forty studies and statements. Many of its studies have come to be regarded as among the most authoritative analysis of particular bilateral topics, and the Committee intends to continue to devote a substantial portion of its efforts to initiating and supervising such in-depth research. But such research takes a considerable amount of time to do well. In recent years, many bilateral issues have become highly politicized quite quickly, calling for more immediate and continuing comment.

Over the past year the Committee has initiated, on an experimental basis, a series of *Backgrounders* to provide brief, prompt, and factual reports on issues that have arisen, or that are likely to arise, in the relationship. To date, *Backgrounders* have been released on beef trade, Canadian import quotas on eggs, and the dispute over the deletion of commercials on programs picked up from the United States for broadcasting over Canadian cable television facilities.

This monograph marks another new departure for the Committee. The genesis for this new departure can be found in a Statement by the Canadian-American Committee, *The New Environment for Canadian-American Relations*, which was prepared by Sperry Lea, then the U.S. Director of Research for the Committee, and released in September, 1972. The purpose of this report is to provide an integrated review of the current state of bilateral relations. If it meets with success in terms of fulfilling an important need, the Committee plans to issue similar reports on a regular basis in the future, although the Committee is continuing to experiment to find the most effective format for achieving its publications objectives.

The preparation of the report was a joint effort of the Washington and Montreal staffs of the Committee and its sponsoring organizations, the National Planning Association in the United States and the C. D. Howe Research Institute in Canada. Those involved in the writing were Carl Beigie, Theodore Geiger, Norman Mogil, and John Volpe. Guidance and supervision on behalf of the Committee were provided by its Executive Committee, which has approved publication. Since the report is intended to be a factual and descriptive document without specific policy recommendations, it was decided not to take it through the Committee's normal signature process. For Statements by the Committee, signing members are able to register their individual views on particular points through a footnoting procedure.

R. M. MacIntosh
Canadian Co-Chairman

Richard J. Schmeelk
American Co-Chairman

CONTENTS

Tables

1

Introduction

The Canada-U.S. relationship is in a state of transition. Old issues fester, and complicated new problems emerge with disturbing regularity. Thus far, the close formal and informal ties that link the two nations and the underlying bilateral goodwill that exists among the majority of people on both sides of the border have prevented a serious rupture in the relationship. But the current situation can best be described as tense, with little prospect for a near-term resolution of fundamental issues that are straining the relationship from many directions.

The purpose of this report is to review some of the major developments of the past few years that have shaped the current state of the bilateral relationship and to examine the most likely near-term trends and issues in that relationship. In this introduction the theme of difficult transitions is developed and related to a variety of recent bilateral issues. Chapter 2 highlights the main elements of the current economic environment in the two countries and examines how this environment has created short-term transitional problems in such areas as trade, investment, and the rate of exchange. Chapter 3 takes a closer look at private capital flows in terms of both short-term economic factors influencing investment decisions and institutional developments that have affected, or might affect, bilateral capital movements. As an example of issues that have persisted in the Canada-U.S. relationship for many years, the Automotive Agreement of 1965 is examined and assessed in Chapter 4. Certain aspects of bilateral energy relations are reviewed in Chapter 5 to illustrate the type of complex new issues that have been emerging. A brief concluding comment completes the report.

Redirecting the Relationship

Progressively closer links between Canada and the United States since World War II evolved from government policy decisions and, to a much greater degree, from private individuals responding to opportunities and incentives created by natural market forces. As this process continued, Canada's ability to sustain a separate identity from the United States was perceived as a problem by an

1

increasing number of Canadians. The government of Prime Minister Trudeau has sought to mobilize this concern into support for policies that would override the integrative tendencies of natural market forces.

Canadian policies having a bearing on the bilateral relationship are based, at least implicitly, on two hypotheses, neither of which has been subjected to careful research. First, it is assumed that closer economic integration between Canada and the United States necessarily implies greater integration in other areas — cultural, social, and especially political. (Given the asymmetry in the size of the two economies and populations, it is further assumed that the United States would dominate this integrative process.) Second, there is an assumption either that policies aimed at overriding natural market forces will not result in significant costs to the Canadian economy or, if they do, that these costs will be accepted by the majority of Canadians.

In the economic sphere, Canadian policies are being directed towards the objectives of greater diversity in trade relationships, increased ownership and control of domestic economic activity, and improved balance in the sources of domestic economic growth. Trade diversity is being sought through a program of expanding contacts and bilateral undertakings with nations throughout the world, with the most notable, and as yet still very vague, example being Canada's pursuit of a "contractual link" with the European Community.[1] Foreign investment in the form of acquisitions of enterprises in Canada and of expansion by foreign-owned firms into new lines of activity in Canada is being screened by the Foreign Investment Review Agency, established in 1974, to ensure "significant benefits" for Canada.[2] More "balanced" growth is a concept that has not been defined precisely for policy purposes but that essentially means industrial and regional diversity and an upgrading of domestic capacities in a broad range of economic activities. It is the objective of efforts to promote further processing of Canadian resources prior to export; regional and industrial incentive programs; government purchases of equipment from foreign suppliers that are tied to provisions for subcontracting in Canada; and

---

[1] Diversity in trade relations is regarded as a key element in Canada's pursuit of the so-called "third option." This option, based on a strategy of strengthening Canada's economic and other capabilities, was put forward as the preferred course of action, as opposed to the other options of seeking closer integration with the United States or of maintaining the status quo, by Mitchell Sharp, then Canada's Secretary of State for External Affairs, in a 1972 article (see Mitchell Sharp, "Canada-U.S. Relations: Options for the Future," in a special issue of *International Perspectives* [Ottawa: Information Canada, Autumn, 1972]).

[2] There is also a movement under way at the provincial level to restrict purchases by non-residents of recreational and agricultural land, with Prince Edward Island and Saskatchewan taking the lead. The issue is now wrapped up in court cases, with major questions to be resolved concerning the legal authority of provinces to restrict purchase by aliens but not by Canadians living in other provinces.

measures to strengthen Canadian capabilities in areas covering such diverse industries as publishing, finance, advertising, film-making, etc.[3]

There are non-economic dimensions to many of these Canadian policy initiatives. "Cultural nationalism," for example, is one of these dimensions that has emerged in recent actions affecting *Time* Canada and the broadcasting of television programs originating from U.S. stations over Canadian cable systems.[4] In both instances, one of the major stated objectives was to improve Canadian potential in the cultural field by increasing the flow of domestic advertising expenditures to Canadian enterprises. In the case of *Time* Canada, a long-standing exemption to Canada's tax provisions, which had allowed Canadian firms' advertising in *Time*'s Canadian edition as a business expense, was removed early in 1976, resulting in the termination of this special edition.[5] Canadian cable television operators in some areas are now required to delete commercial segments of programs taken off the air from the United States with the objective of diverting the current outflow of advertising dollars away from U.S. border stations. Cultural objectives also underline Canadian-content requirements for domestic radio and television broadcasts and pressures to require cinema chains to devote a certain portion of the year to the showing of Canadian-made films.

Other important developments redirecting the bilateral relationship are even more complex. At one level, provincial initiatives in Canada may be redirecting the relationship more rapidly, or in very different directions, than the federal government would wish to see. Examples that have brought some embarrassment to the federal government include the announcement by the Saskatchewan government that it intends to take over part of that province's potash industry, much of which is currently developed by private, foreign-owned firms, and the decision of the British Columbia

---

[3] Canada and the United States both have a variety of industrial incentive programs, many of which may be working at cross-purposes. One difference between the two countries is that Canada's incentive programs are often put forward as part of an overall "industrial strategy," although the purposes and interrelationships among these programs remain illusive to outside observers. For a review and analysis of recent incentive measures in both countries, see John Volpe, *Industrial Incentive Policies in the Canadian-American Context* (Montreal and Washington: Canadian-American Committee, 1976).

[4] The cable television issue is explored in *Backgrounder*, No. 3, *The Canada-U.S. Border Dispute over Television Advertising* (Montreal and Washington: Canadian-American Committee, December, 1975).

[5] *Time* has decided to continue printing the U.S version of its magazine in Canada with Canadian advertising, with a reduction in rates of about 50 percent (taking into account a reduced number of expected subscribers in the calculation of the rates) for these advertisers. The removal of the tax exemption was coupled with other provisions, based essentially on administrative discretion, that will permit *Reader's Digest* to continue publications of a Canadian edition. Several smaller periodicals were also affected by the removal of the tax exemption.

government in 1974 to suspend natural gas shipments to Washington state under long-term contract without prorationing between domestic and foreign customers.[6]

At a much broader level, changes in international relations are creating a new environment within which decisions by both countries concerning the bilateral relationship must be made and assessed. "Cold War" confrontations have gradually given way to new issues in international relations based more on economic rivalry than on strategic alignments. This environment, in which issues of "fairness" in national and regional economic policies have taken on a greater importance, shapes the perceptions of many people in the United States concerning Canadian initiatives to redirect the relationship.

The U.S. government appears willing to accept Canada's longer-term objectives for the bilateral relationship as inevitable and even understandable. Despite signs of strain over specific "irritants" and despite calls by some Americans for retaliatory action when Canadian measures have been perceived as harmful to U.S. interests, the U.S. government has stressed the importance of consultation rather than to threaten countermeasures. Still, the United States has contributed, and may even have sparked, the redirection exercise. It has refused in recent years to differentiate its policies to accommodate Canada's claims for special treatment with respect to the temporary import surcharge imposed in mid-1971 and the DISC tax legislation passed later that year; and it adopted a strict interpretation of U.S. law regarding countervailing duties when it imposed a modest penalty on exports of Michelin tires from Canada to the United States on the grounds that these exports received an unfair "bounty or grant" in the form of inducements to production from the federal and provincial governments.

Even though both governments continue to claim that bilateral relations are essentially cooperative and friendly, issues are accumulating during a transitional process that both sides would like to see take place gradually and with as little hostility as possible. Three types of problems illustrate the difficulties inherent in this longer-term transition.

First, because the Canadian government is attempting to override natural market forces tending to advance the degree of North American integration, its policies must be interventionist. The U.S. government, in contrast, at least under Presidents Nixon and Ford, has supported a philosophy that is far more market-oriented. (It is indicative of differences in economic philosophies that Mr. Ford is pressing for "deregulation" of many government controls at the same

---

[6] In the potash case, there is concern in the United States that provincial government ownership will affect the availability of potash exports, and a resolution has been passed by a group of senators calling on the U.S. Administration to seek Canadian assurances on supply access.

time that Mr. Trudeau is indicating that new forms of long-term government controls may be necessary following the current wage and price measures, now scheduled for removal at the end of 1978.) An example of the kinds of issues that can arise from different attitudes towards market forces is provided by the Automotive Agreement (discussed in Chapter 4), where negotiations for changes in its terms have reached an apparent impasse because the U.S. position is based on the goal of greater market freedom whereas the Canadian position is to seek new undertakings to regulate the market. Other types of issues in this area are illustrated by the recent case of Canadian import quotas on eggs.[7]

Second, there is a fine line between upgrading a nation's capabilities, on the one hand, and protectionism, on the other. That line is determined as much by perception as by fact. There are currently serious challenges in the international economic system to trade liberalization, "fair" trade, and multilateralism. The United States, as one of the major proponents of an open world trading system, is being watched closely by other nations not only in terms of its own actions but also in terms of the principles it adopts in its trade relations with other nations, including Canada.

Third, there has been a move away from bilateral policy initiatives of the type that create potential advantages to both sides (the Automotive Agreement would be an example of such an initiative, as would the Defence-Production-Sharing Agreement; energy swaps, discussed briefly in Chapter 5, would be a possible example for the future). Issues are now being examined separately from one another, and it is virtually impossible politically for the Canadian government to appear to be giving up something to the United States, even if in return for a broader agreement bringing greater benefits. It is unrealistic to think that issues can continue to accumulate in which Canada's perceived gains are achieved at the expense of someone in the United States (as in the cases of *Time* Canada, cable television, oil export cutbacks, the potash takeover, etc.) without resentment mounting and pressures for retaliatory actions by the U.S. government increasing.

Even with the best of intentions and with basic understanding between the two governments, issues of the sort raised here make difficult the longer-term transition now taking place as a result of Canadian attempts to redirect the relationship.

Process of Economic Recovery

The outlook for bilateral relations over the next few years is likely to be affected significantly by the process of recovery from the

---

[7] See *Backgrounder*, No. 2, *Canada's Import Quotas on Eggs: A Case of Domestic Goals Versus International Relations* (Montreal and Washington: Canadian-American Committee, September, 1975).

sharp economic downturn of 1974-75. Both countries face difficult transitions from high inflation and high unemployment to reasonably full employment with improved price stability, but at the present time the tasks facing Canada appear to be the more difficult. Because the economic downturn was less severe in Canada than in the United States, the above-average productivity gains that normally accompany an economic recovery will be harder to achieve in Canada; while Canada's trade performance can be expected to improve (especially in the automotive and resource sectors) as the U.S. and other major economies pick up, its current account balance is likely to remain in substantial deficit this year and probably next; and the full consequences of changes in comparative wage costs, with Canada's rising faster than those in the United States, may take several years to unfold.

The exchange rate is presenting Canada with some particularly perplexing problems. As of the early spring of 1976, the Canadian dollar was trading at a modest premium in relation to the U.S. dollar in the spot (for immediate delivery) market, representing an appreciation of nearly 10 percent in relation to the U.S. dollar since early 1970, just prior to the time it was allowed to "float." Yet over this same period, there was a deterioration in Canada's overall trade account of nearly $3 billion. Furthermore, the "gap" between Canadian and U.S. manufacturing wages has essentially been eliminated, while a substantial productivity differential remains, putting Canada in a less competitive position. (This point is discussed further in Chapter 2.)

High interest rates in Canada are encouraging capital inflows into Canada and keeping the exchange rate for the Canadian dollar strong. In the short run, at least, capital inflows will continue to be necessary to finance Canada's current account deficit, even if the exchange rate should fall. (It takes time for a lower exchange rate to show up in an improved trade performance.) These capital inflows, when they come in the form of purchases of Canadian debt, create future interest obligations on a fixed schedule, and these obligations have to be met by either higher foreign exchange earnings or additional borrowing. To complicate matters further, even if the Canadian dollar were to fall in value, import prices paid by Canadians would rise, adding to future inflationary problems.

Looking at the near-term economic outlook in Canada, then, it is reasonable to expect some combination of the following to occur:

• The need to sustain capital inflows will allow limited scope for independent Canadian monetary policy. Furthermore, equity capital may have to be sought, or at least not rejected, both to meet capital financing needs and to relieve the pressure from mounting fixed commitments for debt servicing.

• Canada will have to seek whatever export markets can be found, and this will probably mean a continuing reliance of primary-product exports, with manufacturing exports having to struggle to overcome comparative cost handicaps.[8]

• The value of the Canadian dollar will eventually come under downward pressure if interest rates begin to decline relative to those in the United States and abroad. It will be difficult to determine what new level for the exchange rate would be appropriate until the impact of differences in recent Canadian and U.S. economic performance works itself out.

Some of the topics examined briefly in this section will be explored more fully in the next two chapters. In terms of this general introduction, however, it should be noted that some of the basic objectives Canada is seeking to achieve through its attempts to redirect the relationship are going to be difficult to realize because of the problems associated with the process of economic recovery outlined above. A major uncertainty at the present time concerns how the Canadian government will respond to this situation.

Decisions Affecting Shared Resources

Many of the most important issues in Canadian-American relations concern the use of resources that are shared. These include rivers that flow across the boundary and migratory fish and fowl. On occasion these issues emerge as major news items — such as the Garrison Diversion Project in North Dakota, which is anticipated to affect water quality of the Souris River in Canada adversely, and the proposal to raise the water level behind the Ross Dam in Washington state, flooding land in the Skagit Valley in Canada — but both countries have fully recognized their common interests and mutual obligations in these issues. Well-tried procedures have been adopted for settling disputes, with a leading role being played by the International Joint Commission, an advisory and research group appointed by both countries but with a responsibility for independence.

The purpose of citing the example of the decision-making process and the approaches adopted in the area of shared resources is to close this introduction on a positive note. When common interests are clearly perceived, difficult transitions can be accommodated.

---

[8] Concern over export prospects and the balance of payments was the major reason why Canada dropped controls on export profits from its anti-inflation program in late February. Provincial governments were especially insistent that this decision be taken.

2

The Current Economic Environment

The past several years have been a period of exceptional instability as the international community has had to contend with major disruptions to the traditional economic order. Serious troubles began to emerge in 1972-73, when there was a simultaneous upturn in all the major economies, producing one of the most rapid and broadly based expansions in modern economic history. The pace of the expansion proved to be more than the world economic system could sustain. Shortages emerged in virtually all commodities, and prices of industrial raw materials and basic foodstuffs surged upward, reaching peaks as much as three and four times their previous levels. Coming on top of inflationary pressures that had been building up for several years, these strains were simply too much for the system to cope with, and the basis for "double-digit" inflation was laid.

The finishing blow came in late 1973 and early 1974, when oil supplies were disrupted and then the world price of oil was raised suddenly and dramatically by the OPEC cartel. Faced with unacceptably high rates of inflation and severe balance of payments deficits resulting from higher oil import bills, the major nations of the world were unable to prevent economic stagnation and decline. In consequence, the world entered a recession that lasted throughout most of 1974 and 1975, producing the worst economic downturn of the postwar period.

Inflation has recently begun to moderate, and recovery appears to be taking hold in most of the major economies. But this recovery is likely to be fragile in 1976, with nations treading cautiously for fear of a renewal of inflationary pressures. Full recovery will be a protracted process, since the instabilities of the past several years have created imbalances that will not be easily corrected.

Rapidly changing economic conditions have forced nations everywhere to adjust to new and difficult conditions under which trade and investment must take place. It is within this general context that Canada and the United States have had to re-examine their domestic and international policies and their relations with each other. The purpose of this chapter is to examine how these developments have affected bilateral trade patterns, financial flows, and the relationship between the two currencies and to examine likely trade trends in the near-term future.

Changes in the Bilateral Trade Balance

Canada's current account deficit with the United States, including trade in goods, services, and other "invisible" transactions such as interest payments, has increased sharply over the past several years. It has grown from $840 million in 1973 to $1.5 billion in 1974 to $4.6 billion in 1975.[1] The deficit in 1975 was by far the largest ever recorded. This deterioration reflected a change from surplus to deficit in Canada's merchandise trade with the United States (shown in Chart 1), and a further increase in the deficit on service transactions. Canada's current account deficit with all countries exceeded $5.5 billion in 1975, creating a much-discussed policy issue.

The turnaround in the bilateral trade account is explained by two main factors:

Fluctuations in world commodity prices. Canada's trade account was given a substantial boost in 1973 as world prices for many key industrial raw materials took off in late 1972 in response to the exceptional expansion in industrial activity worldwide. Between 1972 and 1974 Canada's terms of trade — the average price of exports in relation to the average price of imports — increased by 19 percent, largely on the strength of the worldwide run-up in commodity prices during this period.[2] However, since the middle of 1974 the rapid fall-off in world commodity prices has reversed this trend.

Divergent cyclical patterns of economic growth in Canada and the United States. In 1974 Canada experienced real, albeit modest, gains in national income, all registered in the first several months of the year. By comparison, the U.S. economy recorded a decline in real national income of 2.2 percent, the first such decline in more than two decades. Besides this overall better growth performance, there are a number of other important features that distinguish Canada's cyclical pattern from the U.S. pattern and hence help explain the timing and extent of the swing in the bilateral trade balance:

• Economic growth in Canada stalled in the second half of 1974 but did not turn negative until the beginning of 1975; the U.S.

---

[1] There has always been a considerable discrepancy between Canadian and U.S. reporting of the bilateral current account balances. In general, U.S. figures on merchandise trade account show a larger Canadian deficit, but the basic trend is essentially the same as shown in the Canadian statistics used throughout this chapter. Canadian and U.S. official statistics are compared in an appendix to this chapter.

[2] Calculations based on data given in Statistics Canada, *National Income and Expenditure Accounts*, Table 21.

CHART 1

**Canada's Merchandise Trade Balance with the
United States, 1973-75, by Quarters, Seasonally Adjusted**
(million Canadian dollars)

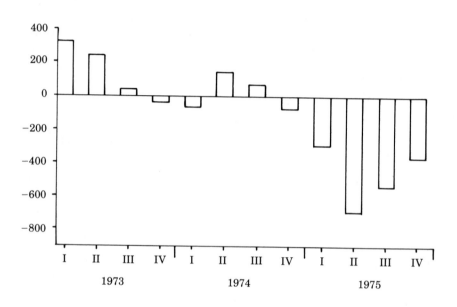

		Canadian Exports	Canadian Imports	Balance
1973	I	4,103	3,769	335
	II	4,233	3,967	226
	III	4,202	4,167	35
	IV	4,533	4,581	−48
1974	I	4,888	4,966	−78
	II	5,110	4,993	117
	III	5,679	5,608	71
	IV	5,648	5,738	−90
1975	I	5,273	5,572	−299
	II	5,073	5,782	−709
	III	5,481	6,040	−559
	IV	5,753	6,127	−374

Source: Statistics Canada, *Summary of External Trade*, various issues.

economy, on the other hand, had already fallen off sharply early in 1974 and continued to slide during all of that year and into 1975.

● In cumulative terms, Canada's cyclical downturn was much less severe than that of the United States. At the bottom of the recession the level of real GNP in the United States had fallen 8 percent from the previous peak, while Canada's decline was only 2 percent.

● In specific areas of economic activity, the Canadian economy was being shored up by advances in private investment (5.1 percent in real terms for 1974 over 1973) and by increases in the volume of consumer purchases (4.2 percent). With consumer goods and capital equipment comprising the bulk of U.S. shipments to Canada, the total level of U.S. exports continued to record solid gains during 1974 and into 1975.

An analysis of the composition of bilateral trade flows reveals the presence of both inflation and recession working to shape trade patterns between the two countries. The data in Table 1 focus on Canada's trade balance with the United States in selected commodity groups. Viewed in this way, Canada is shown to have had strong trade surpluses in raw- and semi-processed-material categories (crude and fabricated materials in the table), largely on the strength of price increases in international commodity markets. For example, the value of Canadian exports of crude oil and natural gas to the United States in 1974 was double that in 1973, although the volume of exports actually fell as oil shipments were restricted by the Canadian government. (Canada-U.S. energy relations are reviewed in Chapter 5.)

By comparison, the trade balances in manufactured products (end products in the table) continued to widen in favour of the United States. Part of the widening in this area of the trade balance reflects the enlarged U.S. surplus in automotive trade, which reached a level of $1.9 billion in 1975 (as computed by Canadian statistics).[3] A severe slump in the U.S. new-car market, starting in late 1973, eventually spilled over and adversely affected Canadian production destined for the U.S. market. Excluding automotive trade, the United States has more than doubled its surplus in manufactured products over the past three years, from $3 billion in 1972 to $6.4 billion in 1975, as the stronger economic performance in Canada stimulated the growth of U.S. exports of machinery and equipment.

---

[3] Three different estimates of the bilateral trade balance in automotive parts are available in the United States. First, the *Annual Report of the President to the Congress on the Operations of the Automotive Products Trade Act of 1965* employs Canadian import data; this estimating procedure, which is officially used by both governments, indicates that the U.S. trade surplus amounted to $1.9 billion in 1975. Second, the Balance of Payments Division of the U.S. Department of Commerce,

(cont'd on page 12)

TABLE 1

**Canada's Trade Balances with the United States,
by Major Commodity Group, 1972-75**
(million Canadian dollars)

	1972	1973	1974	1975
Live animals	27	−13	−28	2
Food, beverages	53	0	−332	−396
Crude materials	1,359	1,954	3,953	3,801
Fabricated materials	2,424	2,874	2,822	2,469
End products	−3,053	−4,534	−6,808	−8,326
Excl. autos	−3,051	−4,033	−5,537	−6,421
Automotive[a]	−2	−501	−1,271	−1,905

[a] Computed from different statistics than those used for automotive trade in Chapter 4.

Source: Statistics Canada, *Summary of External Trade*, various issues.

Capital Flows and the Exchange Rate

Capital movements between Canada and the United States, which in 1973 led to a small net flow to the United States, recorded a substantial net inflow into Canada of $2.5 billion in 1974 and then reached an all-time record net flow to Canada of $4.9 billion in 1975. Table 2, which summarizes the bilateral capital account, indicates that both short-term and long-term capital inflows into Canada have risen sharply.

TABLE 2

**Net Capital Movements in Canada's Capital Account
with the United States, 1973-75**
(million Canadian dollars)

	1973	1974	1975
Capital movements:			
In long-term forms	+811	+1,679	+3,214
In short-term forms	−1,123	+811	+1,656
Total net capital balance	−312	+2,490	+4,870

(+) Indicates a net inflow into Canada.
(−) Indicates a net outflow from Canada.

Source: Statistics Canada, *Quarterly Estimates of the Canadian Balance of International Payments*, Fourth Quarter, 1975.

(cont'd from page 11)

using U.S. export and import figures, reports a U.S. surplus of $1.1 billion. Finally, the U.S. Bureau of the Census, which employs quite different estimates for U.S. exports and imports, shows that the U.S. surplus amounted to only $800 million.

The main factor behind the change in the long-term capital account was an increase of $3.4 billion in net new issues of Canadian bonds sold in the United States during 1975. Provincial borrowing, which accounted for the vast majority of this inflow, was in response to sharply rising financial requirements, especially by crown corporations. In addition, the record level of Canadian placements was a direct result of the widening of the long-term interest differential between Canada and the United States, which averaged close to 3 1/2 percentage points higher in Canada's favour by the close of 1975 (a postwar record), compared to a 2.0 percentage point spread at the end of the previous year. In other areas of the long-term capital account, Canadian direct investment in the United States fell by $133 million between 1974 and 1975.

Short-term rates had a significant impact on bilateral short-term capital movements, which changed from a net outflow from Canada of $1.1 billion in 1973 to a net inflow of $1.7 billion in 1975. Early in 1974 the Canadian short-term interest rate was nearly 2 percentage points below the U.S. rate, but a steady climb in the Canadian rate resulted in the disappearance of the spread by late 1974. By the end of 1975 the spread had reached about 3.0 percentage points (see Chart 2).

Finally, although the Canadian dollar did appreciate by 4 percent in the United States early in 1974, Canada's deteriorating current account (bilaterally and multilaterally) weakened the exchange rate, and, on balance, the Canadian dollar wound up close to parity with the U.S. dollar at the end of the year. However, the continuation of the deterioration in the current account during 1975 did not affect the Canadian dollar adversely. Rather, the high rate of capital inflows during the latter part of 1975 pushed the Canadian dollar to parity and slightly beyond, where it currently rests.

Outlook

Looking to 1976 and a little beyond, there are signs that the factors that previously contributed to economic uncertainty and instability in the international community are gradually receding. The process of economic growth is taking hold in most industrially advanced countries, although the road to full economic recovery will probably be long and arduous. A return to full-employment levels of output will be delayed until at least 1977, and probably later. On the inflation front, most countries have experienced a noticeable improvement in the rate of domestic price advance in comparison with the situation of a year ago. There is a note of optimism beginning to emerge about the ability of national governments to take the steps necessary to bring inflation under control. Still, the threat of a resurgence of inflation is a constant spectre hanging over the international economic community. While oil prices are unlikely to be raised by OPEC sufficiently to introduce a major new thrust to

14

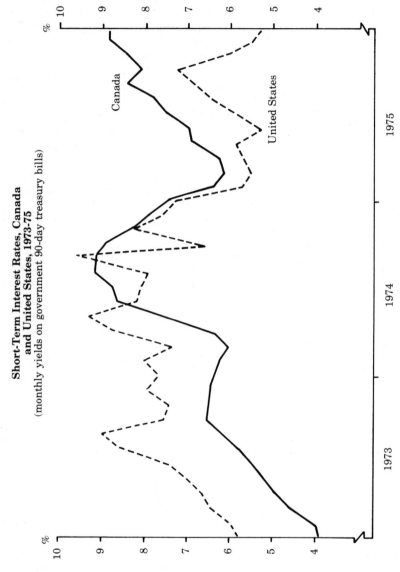

CHART 2

**Short-Term Interest Rates, Canada
and United States, 1973-75**
(monthly yields on government 90-day treasury bills)

Canada

United States

1973   1974   1975

Sources: *Bank of Canada Review* and *Federal Reserve Bulletin*, various issues.

inflationary pressures, the prices of many other commodities have been depressed, probably temporarily, by the recent global recession. The test that lies ahead is to so manage economic policies during the current recovery that progress on inflation is sustained. If this test can be met successfully, a more stable environment will be created in which international trade and investment could be expected to expand steadily over the course of the next twelve to eighteen months at least.

The volume of two-way trade between Canada and the United States will expand as their respective economies gather steam during 1976. However, there is considerable uncertainty about how much change there will be in the bilateral trade account balance. Given that the U.S. economy will probably be growing somewhat more rapidly than the Canadian economy for at least the first two or three quarters of 1976, the trade balance should improve in Canada's favour, with good gains in automotive products and in primary products other than energy. Offsetting this trend will be a continuation in the reduction of Canadian oil, and possibly even natural gas, exports to the United States.

Two other interrelated factors must also be taken into account:

Domestic wage developments. It is now well-documented that Canadian wages in the manufacturing sector have reached, and in many instances surpassed, wage levels for U.S. workers in comparable industries.[4] This development has generated increasing concern in Canada in view of the fact that output per worker in the Canadian manufacturing sector still remains, on average, substantially below levels achieved in the United States.[5]

Comparative productivity performance. Wage increases by themselves do not provide adequate information for an assessment of future trade patterns; there must also be some consideration given to the future course of productivity developments. The United States is expected to reap greater productivity gains than Canada as both countries start their economic recoveries. Having suffered through

---

[4] In a recent study, Barbara Goldman and Judith Maxwell point out a number of measurement problems that arise from a comparison of Canadian and U.S. wage developments. Despite the fact that there is no one single measure of the Canada-U.S. wage gap that is universally accepted, all available measures unmistakably point to a definite narrowing of the gap in favour of Canadian workers. One widely used measure, average hourly earnings in manufacturing (excluding fringe benefits), has the Canadian worker earning $5.11 compared to $4.85 earned by his U.S. counterpart in the third quarter of 1975. In such industries as textiles, minerals, and paper, the spread in favour of the Canadian worker is even wider (see Barbara Goldman and Judith Maxwell, "Confronting the Change in the Canada-U.S. Wage Gap," in Judith Maxwell, ed., *Policy Review and Outlook, 1976* [Montreal: C. D. Howe Research Institute, 1976]).

[5] R. J. Wonnacott estimates that productivity differences amounted to 21.3 percent in favour of U.S. manufacturing workers in 1974 (see *Canada's Trade Options*, Economic Council of Canada [Ottawa: Information Canada, 1975], Table 15-2).

one of the most severe recessions in decades, U.S. industries will have considerably more excess capacity to call upon during the recovery process than will Canada. The result should be a better near-term productivity performance in the United States.

The combination of lower wage gains and the potential for better productivity growth over the near term in the United States than in Canada, leading to a further improvement in the competitive position of U.S. manufacturing in the North American market, was clearly a major concern underlying the decision of the Canadian government to impose wage and price controls on October 13, 1975.

The outlook on the wage front will depend in part on the success of the Canadian controls program, although many commentators in Canada believe that inflationary pressures would have been subsiding in 1976 in the absence of controls. Another critical question, however, concerns wage patterns in the United States. U.S. workers have experienced a significant drop in their real disposable incomes in recent years, and they can be expected to try to improve their positions in collective bargaining this year and next year as the pace of the U.S. economy quickens.

Even if Canadian and U.S. wages reverse the trends of recent years, with U.S. wages rising somewhat faster than Canadian wages, it is unlikely that the situation will soon be restored to what it was prior to the inflationary disruptions of recent years, and this probably means that some downward adjustments will ultimately be necessary in the relative value of the Canadian dollar. The problems this raises for Canada have been outlined in Chapter 1; the way these developments relate to the outlook for bilateral investment flows is the subject of the next chapter.

Appendix to Chapter 2

Reconciliation of Bilateral Trade Statistics

There are significant differences in the Canada-U.S. trade balance as reported in the official statistics of each country. Given the large volume of bilateral trade flows, the tremendous number of individual transactions across the border, and the different reporting agencies involved, some discrepancies in the two countries' published trade statistics are inevitable. By 1971, however, with concern in the United States about its large trade deficit at a high level and with Canada appearing to account for a significant portion of that deficit, these discrepancies had become a bilateral trade issue.

In an effort to determine the major causes of the discrepancies, Canadian and U.S. government statisticians began a project in 1971 to reconcile their respective statistics on bilateral merchandise trade. Table A.1 shows the bilateral trade balance as reported by the two countries and illustrates how large the discrepancies have become (exceeding $2.3 billion in 1974). The results of the reconciliation exercise are also reported in Table A.1, and it can be seen that the reconciled figures depart significantly from those given in either country's national statistics. National perceptions still tend to be formed by these national statistics.

TABLE A.1

**Canada's Merchandise Trade Balance with the United States,
1970-74: Reconciliation of Bilateral Trade Data**
(million U.S. dollars)

	1970	1971	1972	1973	1974
Canadian figures	+1,036	+1,072	+1,014	+566	+4
U.S. figures	+2,008	+2,326	+2,492	+2,611	+2,350
Reconciled figures	+1,424	+1,450	+1,548	+1,221	+928

Sources: Statistics Canada, *Canadian Statistical Review*, April, 1974, p. 4; Statistics Canada, Press Release, May 21, 1975.

When U.S. and Canadian trade officials began to examine the reasons for the differences in the national statistics, the principal problems were found to lie in complex technical factors arising from the somewhat different conceptual frameworks used in the two countries' trade accounts. For example, the U.S. definition of merchandise trade had to be modified to achieve a reconciliation by adding sales and purchases of military goods and by crediting to Canada goods received in Canada and then re-exported to the United States. (Standard U.S. practice credits these goods to the country of origin.) For Canada, the reconciliation process required that transactions with U.S. possessions (e.g., Puerto Rico) be added to the bilateral ledger. Other discrepancies arose in the treatment of "errors and omissions" and in the lack of synchronization of exchange rate conversions during periods of rapidly changing currency values.

The resulting adjustments to the merchandise trade account figures involve other, offsetting adjustments in various components of the total balance of payments. Unfortunately, these adjustments are published only after considerable delay.[1] To date, the reconciliation exercise has focused on the current account of the bilateral balance of payments (which includes goods, services, interest payments, etc.). The two countries have now begun to extend their reconciliation efforts to the bilateral capital account (which reports various types of investment flows).

---

[1] For a discussion of the adjustments made to the 1970 bilateral current account balance, see Caroline Pestieau, *A Balance of Payments Handbook* (Montreal and Washington: Canadian-American Committee, 1974), Chap. 3, Appendix.

3

Factors Affecting Bilateral Private Capital Flows

Economic, political, and institutional developments are creating new, and largely unpredictable, influences on private capital flows between Canada and the United States. So long as its current account remains in substantial deficit, Canada must rely upon net capital inflows to achieve balance in its international transactions.[1] These net inflows, however, may take a variety of forms and come from investors anywhere in the world. Furthermore, net total inflows may be the result of much larger gross capital movements in both directions and even of net outflows in particular classes of investment. Investor decisions are affected by a different set of factors for each type of investment. The purpose of this chapter is to examine some of the key factors involved in terms of changes having a potential impact on bilateral capital flows.

Economic Developments

The first two chapters of this report have outlined a number of economic developments in Canada and the United States that can be expected to have a bearing on various types of capital flows. The most important among these are wage rates, productivity performance, interest rates, and the rate of exchange. We will examine the possible impact of these developments on three types of capital flows — acquisitions of equity shares, direct investment in productive assets, and investment in fixed-income securities.

People purchase equity shares in foreign companies for the dividends and capital gains (adjusted for any anticipated exchange rate changes) they expect to receive. Thus profitability and growth

---

[1] Reductions in international reserves (gold, foreign currencies, etc.) can be used as a balancing item. In early 1976, however, Canada was in the curious position of accumulating reserves despite a huge current account deficit. These reserve acquisitions, which kept the Canadian dollar from rising to a further premium relative to the U.S. dollar, were necessitated by massive capital inflows arising from relatively high Canadian interest rates.

prospects are the essential determinants of this type of investment decision. Prospects are that growth during the current recovery will be more rapid in the United States than in Canada, thereby generating a somewhat better outlook for capital gains in the former, at least in the short run. A similar situation appears likely in terms of profitability — and thus dividends — since U.S. productivity performance is expected to outpace that in Canada because of the fact that the recession was significantly more pronounced in the United States. Strictly on economic grounds, therefore, conditions over the near term would appear to favour the United States over Canada for investment in equity shares. This conclusion does not, of course, necessarily apply to all industries and firms. For investors having a long-term horizon, there would not appear to be any clear economic rationale for judging prospects as being superior in one country or the other.

Decisions regarding direct investment in productive assets are far more complicated. To simplify matters, let us consider a situation in which an investor originally had no strong preference for locating in one country as opposed to the other. The sharp rise in Canadian wages relative to those in the United States in recent years would clearly now tend to cause that investor to prefer a location in the United States, provided that the current wage relationship was expected to persist and the Canadian dollar was not expected to decline in relation to the U.S. dollar. In resource-intensive industries, these wage developments would be less significant than in labour-intensive industries. In general, however, it would appear reasonable to expect that foreign direct investment in Canada is going to be restrained in relation to that in the United States, at least until the wage and exchange rate outlook is clarified.

From the standpoint of a nation's balance of payments, investments in fixed-income securities essentially play a residual, or balancing, role, with interest rate policies having a dominant role in influencing the magnitude of these flows. In the Canada-U.S. context, relatively high Canadian rates of interest generally tend to attract capital inflows. At the short-term end of the market, these inflows mainly reflect investments by Americans seeking the highest rate of return available; at the long-term end, they mainly reflect borrowing by Canadians seeking the lowest cost of capital available. Also, American lenders of short-term funds usually receive a claim (in terms of both principal and interest) in Canadian dollars; Canadian borrowers of long-term funds usually acquire a liability (again in terms of both principal and interest) in U.S. dollars.

What this all means is that short-term capital inflows into Canada are highly sensitive to expectations regarding the rate of exchange for the Canadian dollar. An American investor can protect himself against the risk of exchange rate changes by purchasing

U.S. dollars with Canadian dollars now for delivery in the future, and the normal situation would be for the terms of this future transaction to reflect, and eventually to offset, differences in short-term interest rates.

The situation has not been normal in the area of bilateral capital flows in recent months. Short-term rates in Canada have risen to a level more than 3 percentage points above those in the United States (see Chart 2), and a large inflow of U.S. funds to take advantage of this rate spread has made it very expensive to protect against the risk of decline in the value of the Canadian dollar through transactions in the forward market. What has been happening is that many investors have been placing short-term funds in Canada on an "uncovered" basis, betting that the Canadian dollar will not decline by anywhere near as much as the forward discount on the Canadian dollar would imply.

Another unusual element in recent capital flows has been the heavy amount of long-term borrowing by provinces and their agencies in foreign capital markets, especially in the United States. While the gap between long-term interest rates in Canada and the United States has not been as large as the short-term differential, the provinces and their agencies have been attracted by the ready availability of funds in foreign capital markets at a time when provincial borrowing requirements have been large. There are many reasons to believe that part of this borrowing reflects a temporary bunching of new issues timed to take advantage of the availability of foreign funds.[2] Nevertheless, the combination of short-term and long-term capital inflows during the fall of 1975 and early 1976 led to a significant appreciation in the Canadian dollar at a time when the annual current account deficit was in the $5 billion to $6 billion range.

This state of affairs creates some serious instabilities in the Canadian economic outlook. If the value of the Canadian dollar were to decline in international currency markets, as it should, judging from Canada's current account deficit, investors in short-term assets might quickly change their perceptions about the exchange rate risk, resulting in a cutback in capital flows to Canada and the possibility of an accumulation of exchange rate pressures. It should also be noted that, as the exchange rate declines, the cost to Canadian borrowers of interest on long-term debt funds acquired in the United States would increase in terms of Canadian dollars.

Canada has very few options to continued dependence upon interest-rate-sensitive and exchange-rate-sensitive inflows of capital until its current account balance and/or its relative attractiveness to

---

[2] For example, Hydro Quebec was able to raise about $1 billion in a private placement in the first quarter of 1976, thereby covering the bulk of its financial needs for the whole year.

direct investors and purchasers of equity shares improve. As long as the current situation persists, various forms of intervention in currency markets to prevent too rapid a decline in the value of the Canadian dollar can be anticipated.

Institutional Developments

There have been two recent institutional developments in Canada — wage and price controls and the Foreign Investment Review Act — that could have an impact, of uncertain magnitude, on bilateral capital flows.

Canada's anti-inflation program has a general impact in terms of how investors evaluate growth and profitability prospects in that country; it has a specific impact on the near-term attractiveness of the equity shares of Canadian firms. Dividend payments are essentially frozen under the program, although it has been announced that this provision will be reviewed at the end of the first year and exceptions are possible for firms needing new capital. One would expect that, during the period of the freeze, equity shares in Canadian firms are not going to be as attractive to foreign, and Canadian, investors as equity shares in the United States, reinforcing earlier conclusions based on economic developments.

The impact of Canada's Foreign Investment Review Act is difficult to determine. The agency responsible for administering this act has thus far had a record of permitting a large majority of investment proposals subject to review to be carried out. However, the impact of this policy on U.S. direct investment in Canada is likely to result less from the decisions of this agency itself than from the perceptions of U.S. investors regarding the real or imagined attitudes of the Canadian government and public towards them. In this respect, there has been a spreading belief in U.S. business circles that U.S. investment is now unwelcome in Canada and will be increasingly discriminated against in the future. This perception has been reinforced by the recent Saskatchewan announcement of plans to take over a large part of the potash industry in that province, an industry in which U.S. business interests are involved, and by an increasingly anti-American tone among nationalistic spokesmen in Canada.

It is too early to determine whether this U.S. reaction is actually deterring investments that would otherwise have been made. Nevertheless, not only are possible direct investors in the United States increasingly expressing such concerns, but also some U.S. institutional investors are beginning to take the view that their purchases of Canadian bonds should be linked in some way to benefits accruing to their own localities or regions from the resulting power, energy, or other public-service investments in Canada.

Political Developments

There is unlikely to be any significant change in U.S. government policies directly affecting the inflow and outflow of private
investment funds. Of the numerous bills proposed in Congress in
recent years dealing with foreign investment in the United States,
the most likely prospect is for the passage of legislation to increase
even further the data collected by the federal government for use in
analyzing the impact on the U.S. economy. The probability is not
very great that the regulatory powers of the government will be
expanded. During the past several months, actual takeovers of U.S.
companies by foreign interests — although vociferously resisted by
the U.S. managements concerned — have not evoked the public
outcry that the mere possibility of such changes created a year or
two ago.

Nor are controls on the outflow of U.S. private investment very
likely in the next year or so in view of the enormous U.S. payments
surplus in 1975. Not only would the surplus have to disappear, but
it would take several years of large deficits to develop a sufficient
concern on balance of payments grounds to justify the reimposition
of controls.

Increasingly in recent years, questions have been raised regarding the costs and benefits to the American economy of providing
tax and other incentives to stimulate the investment of U.S. private
capital abroad. Should a consensus develop that the costs exceed the
benefits, the consequence might be the reduction, or even the aboli-
tion, of these incentives, which in turn would improve the attractiveness of domestic investment compared with foreign investment.
However, such a change in U.S. policy would probably involve a
lengthy legislative process requiring three or four years to complete.

In addition to the institutional considerations noted earlier, U.S.
investment in Canada could be further discouraged by recent comments by Prime Minister Trudeau and certain cabinet members to
the effect that the private market system is not working and may
require more stringent forms of permanent government regulation of
wages, prices, and other aspects of the market economy. If such
views were to be implemented in any really practical ways, it might
well lead to a reduction in U.S. investment in Canada and to a
substantial outflow of Canadian capital funds to the United States.

Another possible development that could significantly affect
government policies, and hence investment flows, between the two
countries relates to the effort of the Canadian government to negotiate a special trade and investment treaty with the European
Community. Until recently, the latter has been decidedly cool to
such an arrangement lest any concessions offered to Canada would
be regarded by the United States as discriminatory, which would
only generate new issues between the Europeans and the Ameri-

cans. However, the negotiations have taken a more favourable recent turn, and there is now a reasonable prospect that an agreement might be reached between Canada and the Community by mid-1976. Such an agreement would be likely to contain little, if anything, of significance in the field of trade because of Community fears of strong U.S. objections and possible retaliation against its exports. In contrast, the Community might be more willing to undertake commitments in the field of investment in return for Canadian assurances of favourable treatment. The reason is that any discrimination thereby involved against U.S. investment would direct U.S. objections, and possible retaliation, against Canada and not against the Community. This possibility, should it materialize, would adversely affect the outlook for U.S. investment in Canada.

Finally, policies affecting capital outflows in both countries may come to reflect increasingly expressed concern about a prospective "capital shortage." The only practical meaning of this term is an expectation that interest rates would be higher than some governmental and private borrowers would be willing to pay. It is by no means certain that interest rates would be lowered by restrictions of capital outflows; in any event, allowing interest rates, adjusted for inflation, to rise would be a good means of attracting an inflow of investment from countries with funds available, thereby relieving the so-called shortage. As noted earlier, Canada really has no effective alternative to such an approach in the near term.

In sum, economic, institutional, and political uncertainties becloud the outlook for investment flows between the two countries during the next year or so. On the basis of prospective economic trends and existing psychological perceptions, the likelihood is that the incentives for U.S. direct and equity-share investment in Canada will not be as strong as those that have generally prevailed during the past thirty years. Conversely, it is possible that the incentives for Canadian investment in the United States could significantly increase, possibly reflecting a much more difficult environment within which U.S. or other foreign subsidiaries in Canada must "make the case" with their parent companies that Canada is a relatively attractive location in which to reinvest existing retained earnings or to attract new direct foreign investment capital funds. Either or both of these developments would reflect and, in turn, would further intensify the issues between the two countries.

In any event, Canada's need to attract net capital inflows to balance its present and prospective current account deficits will probably require substantially higher premiums over U.S. interest rates than have traditionally prevailed.

4

The 1965 Automotive Agreement:
Old Issues Persist

Summary

The Canada-U.S. Automotive Agreement of 1965 is the largest and most complex sectoral trade arrangement ever undertaken between two countries. Throughout its eleven-year history, the Agreement has been the object of criticism and debate, with numerous commentators on both sides of the border claiming that it has produced negative results for their respective countries. The issues that have arisen concerning the Agreement illustrate the problems inherent in any attempt to establish and implement a bilateral trade arrangement that will continue to satisfy both countries over time. In this case the problems have been magnified because of the size and importance of the automotive sector.

What the issues basically come down to is an inability to reach a common understanding about the criteria against which to assess the benefits and costs of the Agreement to each country. The Agreement itself is imprecise in terms of objectives. Stress is placed both on efficiency and on an equitable sharing of the total market of the two countries by each. Yet "equitable" is not defined, and there is no guidance as to what should happen if the goals of efficiency and equity come into conflict, as they often do.

Efficiency is not an easy concept for the general public to understand or for political leaders to promote as the dominant goal of policy-making. Improved efficiency in an industry tends to keep prices down and to raise wages, but it also carries risks that fewer workers will be needed to supply what the customers of that industry want to buy. Furthermore, in an industry with a limited number of large firms and with a heavy concentration of ownership in one of the two countries, there is no simple way of determining, or demonstrating, how the efficiency gains resulting from a bilateral trade arrangement are distributed between, or within, the two countries.

CHART 3

Canada's Trade Balance[a] **on Automotive Products
with the United States, 1965-75**
(million dollars)

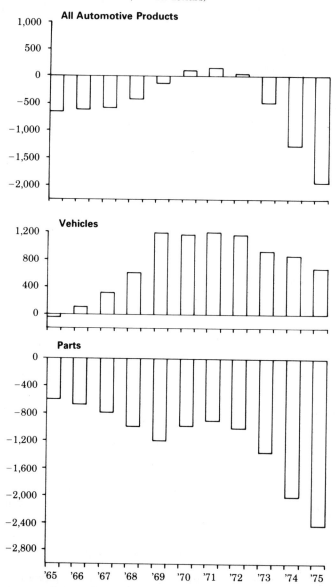

[a] Following an agreement between Canada and the United States that the most accurate measurement of trade could be obtained by comparing the import statistics of each country, Canadian export values are derived from U.S. import statistics.

Source: Statistics Canada, *Daily Bulletin*, various year end issues.

Criticism of the Agreement has focused on the main indicators of its performance in relation to the vague, but politically sensitive, "equitable sharing" objective. From 1965 to 1971 the most visible effect of the Agreement was a significant improvement in Canada's automotive trade balance with the United States (see Chart 3). This improvement was cited by U.S. officials as evidence that Canadian automotive production could, as a result of the Agreement, compete on an equal footing with U.S. production. Therefore, these officials argued, it was time to remove production guarantees — the so-called "safeguards," which the United States maintains were supposed to be transitional in nature — for Canadian automotive manufacturers contained in the Agreement. These guarantees remain an unresolved issue between the two governments.

The improvement in Canada's automotive trade balance with the United States leveled off in 1971-72, and over the next three years the balance plunged into a major deficit position. The dominant cause of this sharp deterioration was a deep slump in automotive sales in the United States at a time when corresponding Canadian sales remained strong (see Chart 4). While Canada's automotive imports from the United States stayed buoyant, its automotive exports to that country fell off substantially. Because of the current large deficit on the bilateral automotive trade account, and a disturbingly large overall current account trade deficit, pressure has been mounting in Canada for the government to negotiate changes in the terms and conditions of the Agreement. The changes that those exerting these pressures have in mind would involve extensions of the "safeguards" now in the Agreement, but this would be in exactly the opposite direction from the U.S. negotiating position regarding the Agreement. Meanwhile, the U.S. government came under additional pressure from those who pointed to the reduction in both output and employment in that country's automotive industry and the Canadian trade surplus in finished vehicles (a surplus that is now being far more than offset by a deficit in parts trade — see Chart 3, panel 3) in support of their claim that Canada is deriving undue benefits from the Agreement.

The future of the Agreement is cloudy as a result of what appears to be a policy stalemate between the two countries on the changes they wish to see made in the Agreement: the United States wants to move closer to an unrestricted free-trade arrangement; Canada wants, or at least is being pressured internally to obtain, additional production guarantees. Either country can pull out of the Agreement upon giving twelve months' notice, but there is a deep reluctance on both sides to take a step that would have such serious consequences. Recovery from the sales slump in the United States, which was proceeding rapidly in early 1976, will bring about a simultaneous improvement in U.S. automotive output and employment and in the Canadian automotive trade balance. Therefore, the

CHART 4

**Volume of New Car Sales in Canada and
the United States, 1966-75**[a]

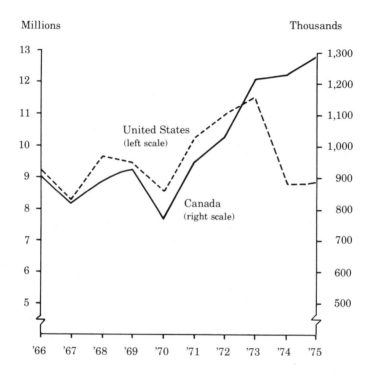

[a] Preliminary estimates for 1975.

Sources: U.S. Department of Commerce, *Survey of Current Business*,
and Statistics Canada, *Canadian Statistical Review*, various issues.

next few years should bring about some lessening of pressures for quick resolution of the current policy stalemate. Looking beyond the recovery, however, there are a number of difficult questions about the future of the North American automotive industry, concerning both the rate of growth of demand and the type of vehicles that consumers will seek, and about the comparative competitive positions of the Canadian and U.S. sectors of the industry. The answers to these questions could produce new strains in the Agreement unless the governments are able to come to terms on possible revisions during the next few years.

The remainder of this chapter is devoted to a brief review of the origins and terms of the Agreement, an assessment of the main effects and issues emerging from it, and a commentary on the recent controversy it has generated. A few observations on the outlook for the Agreement over the next several years conclude the chapter.

Origins and Terms of the Agreement[1]

The Automotive Agreement was negotiated to head off a potentially serious conflict that would probably have emerged from a unilateral Canadian initiative to stimulate the performance of its automotive industry. That industry, protected by a complex system of tariffs and domestic-content provisions, had become burdened by an excessively diversified range of output for a limited home market. Costs and prices were significantly above those in the United States, and the deficit on automotive trade was steadily worsening.

In 1960 a royal commission was appointed to study the industry and to put forward suggestions for overcoming its problems, which were similar to those in most other industries producing major durable goods in Canada. The main recommendation of the commission was that Canadian automotive production should be reoriented towards the international market in order to achieve the efficiency gains that accompany large-scale, less-diversified output.[2] To achieve this result, it proposed that Canadian-content rules, which established the terms under which parts for assembly in Canada could be imported free of duty, should be broadened to include production for export in the determination of content achieved. In October, 1963, following a year's experience with a modest pilot plan, the Canadian government announced a program that would allow its automotive manufacturers to receive full remission of duties on imports of new vehicles and original equipment parts up to the value of Canadian content in exports of new vehicles and original parts over and above

---

[1] For a complete review of the origins, objectives, and earlier effects of the Agreement, see Carl E. Beigie, *The Canada-U.S. Automotive Agreement: An Evaluation* (Montreal and Washington: Canadian-American Committee, 1970).

[2] *Report of the Royal Commission on the Automotive Industry* (Ottawa: Queen's Printer, 1961).

the base level achieved in the period November 1, 1961-October 31, 1962.

Canada's duty-remission plan was challenged in the United States as constituting an unfair "bounty or grant" to promote exports to that country. If this challenge had been sustained, which appeared likely, there would have been an automatic imposition of a countervailing duty under U.S. law (as in the recent case of Michelin tires produced in Canada with the benefit of regional incentives and exported to the United States). Such a decision by the United States would probably have been followed by further Canadian initiatives, setting off a process of retaliation that would have had serious adverse consequences for the bilateral relationship.

It was against this background that negotiations were begun that resulted in the Automotive Agreement of 1965. The Agreement sought to bring about the early achievement of the following objectives:

(a) The creation of a broader market for automotive products within which the full benefits of specialization and large-scale production can be achieved;

(b) The liberalization of United States and Canadian automotive trade in respect of tariff barriers and other factors tending to impede it, with a view to enabling the industries of both countries to participate on a fair and equitable basis in the expanding total market of the two countries;

(c) The development of conditions in which market forces may operate effectively to attain the most economic pattern of investment, production and trade.[3]

These objectives were to be sought through the removal of duties on trade between the two countries in specified motor vehicles and original equipment parts, thereby promoting an integration of the Canadian and U.S. sectors of North American automotive production. But the Agreement stopped short of being a complete free-trade pact. On the U.S. side, a modest restraint was imposed to ensure that third-country producers did not use the Agreement as a device to escape U.S. duties by bringing their products in through Canada.

Much more important restrictions on free trade were imposed by Canada. Duty-free entry was limited to *"bona fide"* Canadian manufacturers; and to classify as *bona fide,* manufacturers had to fulfill certain production criteria contained in the Agreement itself and to assure the Canadian government, through "letters of undertaking," of their intention to increase the value-added content in Canadian automotive production.[4] These conditions, or "safeguards," were in-

---

[3] *Agreement Concerning Automotive Products Between the Government of the United States of America and the Government of Canada,* Appendix A.

[4] The conditions in the Agreement itself require firms to maintain a ratio between vehicle production and sales in Canada at no less than that in the 1964 model year

(cont'd on page 31)

sisted upon by Canada to ensure that the Agreement did not result in the wholesale transfer of its production activities to the United States.

Evaluating the Results of the Agreement

An assessment of the effects of the Automotive Agreement must begin with a recognition of its role in heading off a potentially serious bilateral dispute in this important industrial sector of the two economies. In its absence, Canada's duty-remission plan almost certainly would have been considered a violation of U.S. customs laws, and Canada, intent upon improving its bilateral trade balance in automotive products, probably would have retaliated with further protective measures — for example, imposing import quotas or raising Canadian-content requirements. Such actions would have affected relations between the two countries adversely, with negative consequences for bilateral trade in automotive products, for other indicators of economic performance in automotive and related industries, and for the close ties between U.S. automotive manufacturers and their Canadian subsidiaries.

In terms of clearly positive effects, the Agreement has been highly successful when judged by its stated efficiency objectives and by conventional economic criteria. Automotive products shipments, now the largest single item of trade between the two countries, have grown enormously since the Agreement has been in effect, with preliminary data for 1975 indicating total two-way trade of over $12 billion (see Chart 5). In addition, the Agreement has stimulated both auxiliary U.S. trade with Canada in such products as machinery and equipment necessary for the expansion of Canadian production facilities and automotive exports from Canada to third countries.

The dramatic expansion of bilateral automotive trade reflects and underlines both the substantial increase in the integration of North American automotive production and the improved efficiency of Canadian production. As indicators of the degree to which production decisions are now made with respect to total North Ameri-

(cont'd from page 30)

(August 1, 1963-July 31, 1964), thereby providing long-term protection to the vehicle-assembly sector of the Canadian industry; to provide modest transitional protection to parts production, firms have been required to maintain the dollar value of Canadian content in Canadian-produced vehicles at no less than that achieved in the same 1964 model year. This latter "safeguard" has been eroded nearly to the point of insignificance by inflation and the growth of the market since 1965. The conditions in the "letters of undertaking," which were negotiated in Canada with the manufacturers and were not made public in the United States until after the Agreement was passed, committed producers to increase their value added in Canada by an amount equal to 60 percent and 50 percent of the growth in the net sales value of cars and commercial vehicles, respectively, sold in Canada, *plus* a total of $260 million (Can.) by the end of the 1968 model year. Although the $260 million had to be achieved by the specific date of the 1968 model year, the conditions in the "letters of undertaking" had no fixed termination date.

CHART 5

**Total Value of Canada-U.S. Trade
in Automotive Products, 1966-75** [a]
(billion Canadian dollars)

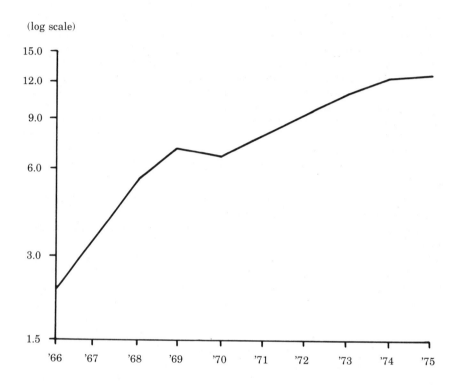

(log scale)

[a] Preliminary estimates for 1975.
Source: Statistics Canada, *Daily Bulletin*, various year end issues.

can needs, approximately 70 percent of all vehicles produced in Canada in 1974 were exported, compared with less than 7 percent in 1964; and imports from the United States comprised about 55 percent of Canada's market for North American-produced vehicles in 1974, compared with less than 3 percent in 1964.[5] In his study of the Agreement, Beigie concluded that major new investments in manufacturing and assembly facilities in Canada had enabled the vehicle producers to exceed the performance required of them by the safeguards as early as 1968. Moreover, the efficiency with which new and modified production facilities in Canada were employed was significantly improved by a sharp reduction in the different lines of vehicles and components turned out and, with the inducements of the Agreement's safeguards and a buoyant North American demand, by greatly increased production runs of those lines selected for specialization.

Thus under the Agreement the Canadian automotive industry has become more efficient *vis-à-vis* its U.S. counterpart.[6] In turn, efficiency gains allowed Canadian manufacturers to meet labour demands for nominal wage parity with U.S. automotive workers beginning in 1970 with no discernible effect on Canadian production. Prior to the Agreement, wages in the Canadian automotive industry were about 25 percent lower than those in the United States. Efficiency gains have also resulted in a reduction in the differential between Canadian and U.S. factory prices for comparable automobiles, from more than 10 percent in 1965 to between 5 and 6.5 percent in 1975, though it should be noted that the actual differential increases for comparable vehicles of larger size and fluctuations in the bilateral exchange rate can obscure changes in the price differential over time. Furthermore, changes in vehicle excise taxes (which have been eliminated in the United States) produce a larger differential in terms of the prices consumers actually pay.

In addition to its effects on the Canadian automotive industry, the Automotive Agreement has also had a dramatic impact on Canada's overall level of output and exports. In one study, it has been estimated that, in the absence of the Agreement and compensating government action, gross national expenditure in 1961 dollars

---

[5] 1974 data obtained from Department of Industry, Trade and Commerce officials; 1964 figures found in Beigie, *op. cit.*, p. 74.

[6] A recent study by the Ontario government suggests that, in assembly operations, Canadian productivity has declined significantly in comparison with U.S. productivity. It is uncertain to what extent this pattern has been affected by cyclical factors, exchange rate changes, and data limitations (there have been major revisions recently to U.S. productivity statistics for the late 1960s and the 1970s), but the study's results have generated considerable comment in Canada. See Budget Paper F, "Performance under the Auto Pact: An Ontario Perspective," *Ontario Budget*, 1976 (Toronto: Ontario Government Bookstore, 1976).

would have been 4.7 percent lower in 1969, and exports of goods and services would have been 21.4 percent lower.[7]

Areas of Controversy Concerning the Agreement

Canada's overall gains from the Automotive Agreement can be documented far more easily than U.S. gains: it now has a larger, more efficient automotive sector; its automotive workers, in contrast with Canadian workers in many other manufacturing sectors, can legitimately point to significant productivity gains over the past decade as a justification for wage parity with their U.S. counterparts; and its consumers have seen the relative premium they must pay over U.S. prices decline, at least after tax and exchange rate differences have been eliminated. Gains have also been realized by the United States, but they must be perceived more in terms of what negative consequences might otherwise have arisen in the absence of the Agreement, especially for the subsidiaries of U.S. firms in Canada.

Despite clear and convincing evidence of efficiency gains from the Agreement, commentary on its effects is dominated by controversy in both countries. This controversy focuses on shares of total trade, employment, and capital investment, and it has now grown sufficiently intense that the two governments are under considerable pressure to renegotiate the terms of the Agreement.

Controversy in Canada has arisen mainly in the areas of the automotive trade balance, price differentials, and the shift in decision-making power over what happens in the Canadian automotive industry to the United States. This latter point is difficult to take seriously, since U.S. subsidiaries were already dominant in Canada prior to the Agreement and decision-making in any event was severely circumscribed by the inefficient environment within which these subsidiaries operated. The controversy over prices will be taken up briefly later in the context of future policy options. Therefore, we concentrate here on the balance-of-trade issue.

During the eleven-year life of the Agreement, Canada has had a cumulative automotive trade deficit with the United States of more than $5 billion. The deficit for 1974 was $1.2 billion, and preliminary estimates place the deficit at $1.9 billion for 1975 (Canadian data sources), more than twice what it was at the time the Agreement was negotiated. The magnitude of the recent deficits has been the result of a sharp slump in U.S. automotive sales (a slump

---

[7] See D. Wilton, "An Econometric Model of the Canadian Automotive Manufacturing Industry and the 1965 Automotive Agreement," *Canadian Journal of Economics*, Vol 5., No. 2, May, 1972, pp. 157-81. While compensatory moves would almost certainly have been taken by the Canadian government had the Agreement not been in effect, unilateral initiatives alone would be most unlikely to have had the same positive efficiency effects.

that was not observed in Canada — see Chart 4), and recovery of these sales will improve the Canadian trade position. Still, these large deficits have generated concern, for three reasons.

• They have contributed to a very severe overall current account deficit in Canada's foreign transactions. This deficit was approximately $5.5 billion in 1975 and is not expected to improve significantly in 1976.

• They reflect a sharp reversal from the trend of steady improvement during the early years of the Agreement.

• They have contributed to Canadian concerns about the future strength of the automotive industry in North America and the ability of Canada to maintain, let alone to expand, its position in this key industry.

Particularly strong criticism of the Agreement in its current format has come recently from the Canadian Automotive Parts Manufacturers' Association, which represents independent parts producers. The Association maintains that the Agreement continues to have an adverse impact on Canada's automotive industry because manufacturers of original equipment parts are unable to obtain an equitable share of the North American market. They contend that this situation has arisen because the Agreement does not encourage the use of domestically manufactured parts for Canadian-produced vehicles; because U.S. vehicle manufacturers are placing a greater percentage of original equipment orders with their Canadian-owned plants and with parts producers in the United States; and because Japanese, Brazilian, and Mexican parts producers have become competitive in the U.S. parts market. The inability of Canada's independent parts manufacturers to acquire a larger share of the continental market is cited as the major reason not only for Canada's steadily worsening bilateral trade deficit in parts and accessories — $2.1 billion in 1974, approximately $2.5 billion in 1975, and about $12 billion since the Agreement was signed — but also for declining capital investment and high levels of unemployment in the country's parts industry. Additional factors mentioned by the Association include higher interest rates in Canada, legislative actions such as the Foreign Investment Review Act, which have discouraged expansion in Canada by U.S. parent companies, and the disappearance of an earlier exchange rate advantage and the existence of nominal wage parity, which have created a less favourable competitive climate in Canada.

The Association maintains that while it does not advocate abrogating the Agreement, certain modifications would enable the Canadian parts industry to obtain a "fair share" of the North American market. In this regard, it proposes changing the content regulations to encourage the use of Canadian-manufactured parts in both U.S.- and Canadian-produced vehicles and the establishment of a bilateral commission to prevent either country from incurring excessive automotive trade deficits.

The Association's case can be argued on three technical points.

First, the reported bilateral parts deficit includes service parts, but they are not covered under the Agreement. Therefore, a more accurate picture of the impact of the Agreement on parts trade would be given by examining original parts shipments alone.

Second, and much more important, about 70 percent of the production parts imported by Canada from the United States are re-exported in finished vehicles, whereas the comparable figure for the United States is less than 10 percent. Therefore, published trade statistics do not give the full perspective of the parts balance. (In other words, Canada's surplus on vehicle trade and its deficit on parts trade cannot be viewed as independent of each other.)

Third, despite a persistent deficit in trade with the United States, the Canadian parts industry has, until the recent slump in the United States, registered improved sales under the Agreement. This trend should reappear as demand continues its recovery in the United States, although there is some evidence to suggest that U.S. sourcing decisions may be changing, particularly in favour of importing parts from third-country producers.

A recent study by the Economic Council of Canada has concluded that Canada actually has a fairly substantial cost advantage over the United States in parts production.[8] It also notes that the industry was able, prior to the recent slowdown, to prosper despite the limited protection afforded by the Agreement. While there has been a decline in Canadian parts producers' share of the domestic market since the Agreement has been in effect, this decline has been offset by the gain of a much larger share of the U.S. parts market.

The Association's call for revisions in the terms of the Agreement in order to obtain a "fair share" of the North American parts market is typical of pressures that have been exerted on both sides of the border. As noted previously, these pressures reflect primary emphasis on the distribution of production rather than on efficiency. Efficiency gains create an opportunity for both countries to improve their positions; distributional shifts in the absence of efficiency gains mean that one country's gains come at the expense of the other. Resistance to being on the losing end of such shifts is the main barrier preventing a mutually satisfactory modification of the Agreement.

The controversy over the Agreement in the United States has focused mainly on the continuation of Canadian production "safeguards," which the U.S. government has always contended were to

---

[8] David Emerson, *Production, Location and the Automotive Agreement* (Ottawa: Information Canada, 1975).

be "transitional." A related issue concerns the fact that individual Canadians are still prevented from buying vehicles in the United States and bringing them back without import duty. Removal of this restriction would, it is argued, lower prices in Canada for North American-produced vehicles, thereby improving their competitive position *vis-à-vis* third-country imports and creating increased automotive output and employment in both the United States and Canada.

The official position of the U.S. government has traditionally been that it is prepared to accept whatever trade balance consequences emerge from the Agreement so long as the results are the product of unrestricted trade flows. The United States apparently continues to maintain this position, as is evident in its desire to press on with the elimination of the safeguards even in the face of very large bilateral automotive trade surpluses in recent years.

The controversies on both sides of the border have spawned a number of new analyses of the Agreement. The Canadian government, for example, has established a special task force to review the effect of the Agreement on Canada's automotive industry, as well as a committee under the Department of Industry, Trade and Commerce to consult with both vehicle and parts manufacturers on the Agreement and possible changes in its terms. Also, a bilateral governmental committee has been set up to study the North American automotive industry.

The U.S. International Trade Commission recently issued a report on the Agreement, undertaken at the request of the Senate Finance Committee. This report should help to defuse some issues of little substance (such as the notion that the United States has had to shoulder too much of the burden of higher unemployment and reduced production in the recent U.S. sales slump, despite the large Canadian trade deficit that has emerged in this period). But it also gives support for long-time critics of the Agreement who claim it is too one-sided in Canada's favour. This conclusion may have been predictable, but it adds further weight to an accumulation of pressures.

A development that might have a bearing on the future of the Agreement is that the U.S. Labor Department found last year that 18,000 Chrysler workers were eligible for adjustment assistance — the largest group of workers ever to be so certified — under the U.S. Trade Act of 1974. The request for this assistance came from the United Auto Workers, who argued that Chrysler had increased its percentage of Canadian-produced automobiles while correspondingly reducing the percentage of those produced in the United States, resulting in a much higher unemployment rate for Chrysler's U.S. workers. The UAW also filed for adjustment assistance for 78,000 workers whose unemployment, it was claimed, had also resulted in part from Canadian imports.

The Labor Department's finding in favour of the Chrysler workers' claim for adjustment assistance appears to have been the result of the following formula: after removing the effects of the recession and the energy crisis on U.S. automotive sales, those workers in plants whose domestic production declined while imports increased would receive adjustment assistance. Some of the import competition considered in this formula was no doubt from Europe and Japan, but it seems that what was mainly involved were imports from Chrysler Canada. It is quite conceivable that imports of a particular model from Canada could have increased as a result of the North American recession. This would occur if, as a result of a decrease in demand, Chrysler closed one plant or shut down one model line in the United States and met its entire demand from a Canadian plant. U.S. imports of that model could well increase while consumption, production, and employment were decreasing. To the extent that this had, in fact, occurred, adjustment assistance benefits in the Chrysler case were due to imports uniquely associated with the Automotive Agreement.

There is another development that could have a bearing on the Agreement in the next year or so — Canada's wage and price controls. The principle of wage parity between workers in the Canadian and U.S sectors of the industry is fundamental to the UAW. It could turn out that U.S. workers will be prepared to settle for a benefits package during their negotiations later this year that will fall within the guidelines established for Canadian workers. (Inflation has been running somewhat lower in the United States than in Canada recently.) Still, the Agreement establishes a clear U.S. interest in the Canadian controls program as it applies to this industry, but this interest has not been formally recognized in Canada; indeed, comments by U.S. officials of the UAW concerning the problems that might arise have provoked a sharp negative response from Canadian government officials.

Outlook

It is far easier to identify pressures for changes in the Automotive Agreement than to anticipate what form those changes might take. As with so many long-standing issues between Canada and the United States, problems remain because no easy solution to them exists.

Both countries have an obvious interest in the continuation of a strong recovery in automotive purchases in the United States, which will increase output and employment in the two sectors and help relieve the current Canadian automotive trade deficit. There is also a common interest in having the industry respond to the challenges of sharply higher gasoline prices and changes in consumer tastes so that existing production facilities can be as fully utilized as possible.

There are, however, fundamental issues concerning the Agreement that must be resolved sooner or later regardless of the industry's outlook. The most basic of these issues is whether the Agreement should move towards a removal of all "safeguards" or towards a new set of production understandings that are more symmetrical between the two countries.

It is difficult for trade liberals to accept the notion that production understandings have any long-term role in a trade arrangement. It is just as difficult to accept the notion that there is any real chance that the Canadian government would agree, or would be able to sell the Canadian public, on a completely free trade arrangement in the automotive industry. Fears, even if unfounded, will persist that U.S.-owned firms would not base their production decisions on free-market considerations and/or that Canada would be at a competitive disadvantage if unrestricted free trade were to be permitted.

These fears figure in the issue of vehicle price differentials. The Canadian government has been willing to accept the existence of a premium, diminishing over time, above U.S. prices in the absence of the kind of market test of comparative production costs that could be made only in an unrestricted free trade arrangement. Thus, the price issue, which has been a major source of controversy in Canada, cannot be finally resolved until and unless the Canadian fears about the production and unemployment consequences of unrestricted free trade in automotive products are assuaged.

With a reasonably healthy recovery of U.S. purchases of North American vehicles, the most likely approach to the Agreement will probably be a compromise based essentially on modest changes in the status quo. The exact form of such a compromise cannot be predicted in advance. What can be predicted is that the Agreement will most likely continue to generate controversy.

5

Energy Relations: Major New Challenges

Summary

No area in the broad spectrum of Canada-U.S. affairs has disturbed the relationship in recent years as much as trade in energy. In rather quick succession, the United States was subjected to a series of unilaterial policy measures affecting both the price and the volume of Canadian energy exports. To Americans these actions seemed unfriendly, if not hostile. As a consequence, these Canadian policy initiatives since late 1973 have probably had a profound and long-lasting impact on energy relations in particular and on the bilateral relationship in general.

The origins of this strain in the bilateral relationship can be traced to the fact that both countries are being forced to adjust their overall energy policies to reflect the new realities of energy supply and demand. Canadians are slowly realizing that their resource base is far from infinite and that they need to take a harder look at a variety of resource management policies that will bring supply and demand into better balance over the longer run. On the other hand, traditional U.S. customers for Canadian energy are faced with the task of redeploying their distribution systems as a means of adjusting to a situation of declining Canadian exports.

The purpose of this chapter is to review and comment on current outstanding issues between Canada and the United States in energy trade. The chapter opens with a brief profile of the changes that have taken place in Canada's perceptions of its energy resource base over the past five years. Against this background, specific Canadian export policies affecting both oil and natural gas are explored within the bilateral context. Finally, the chapter closes by pointing out where there are realistic possibilities for bilateral cooperation that would minimize the potentially high costs that can result from the pursuit of separate energy policies.

Changing Canadian Resource Position

Once considered to be an energy-rich nation, Canada has now become a modest net importer of oil, the first time this has happened in about five years. To be sure, this move to a net oil import position has been voluntary in the sense that Canada has deliberately curtailed the volume of exports to the United States and temporarily shut down some production capacity in Alberta in order to supply the extension of the Interprovincial Pipeline which will meet a part of the Montreal refinery requirements.[1]

Yet the voluntary aspects of this energy position will be short-term. Canada now faces the prospect of becoming a large net importer of oil by 1980 unless large new reserves are discovered in areas of easy access (an unlikely event). This dramatic turnabout in Canada's oil position, from a net exporter in 1973 to an increasingly large net importer in the medium-term future, reflects a combination of four factors:

First, on the consumption side, Canada's domestic requirements are expected to grow at a reasonably fast pace over the next decade. The most recent official estimates forecast an increase in oil consumption of between $3\frac{1}{2}$ - 4 percent year through 1985[2] (see top panel of Chart 6). Conservation measures and higher prices could moderate this trend, but the basic fact remains that the domestic capacity to produce from known sources cannot keep up with future energy needs in Canada.

Second, on the supply side, recent exploration programs in the conventional producing areas have been disappointing. The current assessment is that these areas have peaked in their production, after thirty years of development, and no major new oil deposits are expected to be found. Furthermore, while the prospects for oil discoveries in the Canadian Arctic and the Atlantic regions are still promising, there are as yet insufficient volumes to justify exploitation.

Third, even though the prospects in the Arctic and on the east coast are encouraging, these projects are long-term in the sense that their deliveries cannot be anticipated prior to the middle 1980s at the earliest. For one thing, the buildup in reserves in these frontier regions has been very slow, and it now appears as though more time is needed before the construction of a delivery system can be considered. On top of this, additional time will be required to actually construct pipelines and to provide the basic infrastructure.

---

[1] Actually, export allotments in 1975 were not fully taken up by U.S. refiners, a reflection of the existence of cheaper alternatives and a weak economy in the United States.

[2] Energy, Mines and Resources Canada, *An Energy Strategy for Canada: Policies for Self-Reliance* (Ottawa: Supply and Services Canada, 1976).

CHART 6

**Forecast of Demand[a] and Supply of
Oil and Natural Gas in Canada, 1970-90**

CRUDE OIL (thousand barrels per day)

NATURAL GAS (billion cubic feet/year)

[a] Demand forecast assumes average annual growth rate in real GNP of 4.5 percent through the 1980s.

[b] Assumes that oil prices increase relatively faster than the prices of other goods and services until about 1978, when they reach the current international level (about $13 per barrel in Montreal in 1975 dollars). The price of natural gas is assumed to adjust to "commodity-equivalent" value with crude oil by the 1970s. After 1978 all energy prices are assumed to increase at only the general rate of inflation.

Source: Energy, Mines and Resources Canada, *An Energy Strategy for Canada: Policies for Self-Reliance* (Ottawa, 1976), pp. 83-84.

Fourth, as a consequence of the last two factors, the productive capacity, in the case of oil, has just about reached its peak of two million barrels a day and is expected to decline steadily to less than 1.5 million barrels a day by 1985.[3] Any significant increase in production above two million barrels a day will require major new discoveries in conventional producing areas (noted above) or a more extensive development in the Athabasca oil sands. Regarding the latter prospect, there are several physical and technological limits on the pace at which the oil sands can be exploited.[4] At any rate, Canadian domestic energy needs are growing so rapidly that production from the oil sands can be considered as only a modest substitute for the imports that will be needed to meet Canada's medium-term oil needs.

As far as natural gas is concerned, supply prospects from conventional producing areas appear encouraging. Some experts believe that discoveries of new gas reserves in these areas may be much more responsive to the incentive of higher prices than in the case of oil.[5] Furthermore, Canada has discovered major amounts of gas in the Arctic that await the construction of an economically viable means of transportation to meet Canadian needs. Applications for construction of a natural gas pipeline are now before the National Energy Board, but lags in the regulatory process and in settling native peoples' land claims may delay completion of the line, if it is approved, until 1981 or even later.

What clearly emerges from this discussion of Canada's supply and demand balance is that Canada is rapidly entering a period in which its energy supplies will be increasingly scarce and expensive. Over the medium term the options open to Canada for significantly increased domestic production of oil and gas are limited. As for the longer term, the supply potential is more promising and the options are more flexible, but caution is needed. With this profile of Canada's resource position in mind, we can now turn to a review of the major issues that have developed in the bilateral trade in energy.

---

[3] *Ibid.*, Section III, Chap. 4.

[4] On this point see Judith Maxwell, *HRI Observations*, No. 10, *Developing New Energy Sources: The Syncrude Case* (Montreal: C. D. Howe Research Institute, 1975).

[5] In his submission to the National Energy Board's hearings on natural gas, University of British Columbia economist John Helliwell contended that it is possible to increase domestic production of existing reserves. He argued that deliverability can be increased relatively easily by drilling more wells in existing pools. However, this view was not widely shared by others who submitted testimony to the Board (see "National Energy Board's 1974-75 Natural Gas Supply Hearings," *Canadian Public Policy*, No. 3, Summer, 1975, pp. 415-25).

Price of Canadian Oil Exports

Oil shortages in the United States forced up domestic prices there even before the onset of the Arab oil embargo in November, 1973. Since Canadian crude oil prices were tied to prices set in the Chicago market, prices in Ontario and the western provinces tended to increase along with U.S. prices. On September 4, 1973, the Canadian government announced a temporary freeze on the price of domestic oil of $4.00 a barrel. The feeling at that time was that the U.S. shortages did not bear a relationship to Canadian market conditions and thus Canadians should not be forced to pay inflated prices for their own oil.

However, freezing the domestic price created additional problems. For one thing, not all Canadian producers exported to the United States, so that some producers would benefit from the higher U.S. prices while those serving only the domestic market would not be so fortunate. In response to this problem, the Canadian government introduced an export tax on oil shipments to the United States, in effect creating a two-price system.[6]

The export tax is determined by the difference between the delivered price of imported oil into Montreal and the lower, controlled wellhead price of oil in Alberta. Initially, the export tax was set at 40 cents a barrel in October, 1973 (what was then considered to be a significant amount). However, it was not until after the establishment of the two-price system that the Arab oil-producing states announced their embargo and the international price of oil soared. These developments quickly pushed up the export tax to its peak of $6.40 a barrel in February, 1974. Since then the combination of two increases in the Canadian domestic price and increases in the cost of imported oil into Montreal have brought the export tax to its current (April, 1976) level of $4.60 per barrel.

The export tax has created a good deal of irritation in the United States, for two reasons. First, while most agreed that Canada has a right to charge the same price for its exports as it has to pay now for its imports, there have been charges that Canadian oil is the most expensive source of foreign oil coming into the United States. For the most part, this issue revolves around a series of technical matters related to differences in transportation costs and variations in the quality of oil delivered to Chicago, neither of which can be properly reflected in the export tax. Second, some Americans viewed the two-price system as bestowing an unfair trade advantage on Canadian industry. However, in view of the fact that energy consumption constitutes only a small percentage of total production

---

[6] For a detailed discussion of the two-price system and its implications for Canadian policy, see Norman Mogil, "The Role of Two-Price Systems in Canada," in Judith Maxwell, ed., *Policy Review and Outlook, 1975* (Montreal: C. D. Howe Research Institute, 1975).

costs for most manufacturing industries, it is questionable whether Canadian producers really gained a substantial competitive edge. Nevertheless, this issue persists in the bilateral context, although the Canadian domestic wellhead price is scheduled to increase to $9.05 a barrel on July 1, 1976, and to $9.75 on January 1, 1977. (The delivered cost to refineries in Ontario and Quebec will be 80 cents a barrel higher to cover transportation costs.)[7]

The two-price system may soon disappear as Canada's net import deficit widens in the near future. The two-price system was originally established when the volume of exports roughly equaled the volume of imports, thus conveniently allowing the revenues from the export tax to finance the higher costs of imported oil into eastern Canada. Now, however, Canada has become a net importer of oil — the deficit for 1976 is estimated to average 251,000 barrels a day.[8] This has meant that the Canadian government has had to introduce an excise tax on gasoline to help finance the oil import deficit.[9] Thus as Ottawa cuts back on exports to a planned level of 460,000 barrels a day in 1976,[10] it must rely on some sort of internal taxing system to preserve the two-price system or be forced to dismantle the system entirely.

Finally, many of the problems associated with maintaining a domestic price below world levels have been acknowledged by the Canadian government in its most recent policy statement, *An Energy Strategy for Canada: Policies for Self-Reliance*.[11] The federal government advocates that the domestic price move towards international levels, principally to encourage the exploration and development of new energy supplies. However, Ottawa has not taken any definite position regarding the precise speed with which domestic prices should be phased into the world price, preferring to reach a consensus with the producing and consuming provinces. Specifically, the government is concerned with the inflationary repercussions of higher oil prices and the implications for the international competitive position of some Canadian industries. Nevertheless, Canadians cannot anticipate consuming oil much below the world price for much longer; all they can expect to do is to ease the burden of adjustment to higher world prices.

---

[7] All provinces have agreed to a 60-day freeze on retail gasoline and fuel prices after July 1 and January 1, thus temporarily nullifying the effects of the price increases.

[8] *Oilweek*, February 16, 1976, p. 36.

[9] In its budget of June 23, 1975, the Canadian government introduced a 10-cent-per-gallon excise tax to be applied to non-commercial consumption of gasoline.

[10] This figure represents an average for the year as a whole. As of January 1, 1976, crude oil exports to the United States were 510,000 barrels a day. They will subsequently be reduced further, to 385,000 barrels, sometime later in 1976 (see *Gazette* [Montreal] November 21, 1975).

[11] Energy, Mines and Resources Canada, *op. cit.*

Oil Export Cutbacks

Having to pay more for oil is one thing, but being denied full access to energy supplies is a far more complex and serious matter, as Canada's decision to cut back on its oil exports signifies. Simply, the question of sharing dwindling energy resources goes to the heart of bilateral energy issues.

On November 22, 1974, the Canadian government announced a phasing-out program for Canadian crude oil exports to the United States by the early 1980s. Briefly, this decision arises from two basic considerations:

First, as noted in Chart 6, the domestic demand for oil will substantially exceed domestic production capacity before 1980, and this gap is expected to widen during the 1980s. In view of this prospect, Canada could have decided to cut off exports immediately, but chose not to on the grounds that such a decision would extend self-sufficiency by a period of only about two years, while at the same time it would cause serious hardship to refiners in the U.S. Northern Tier states.

Second, like all other nations, Canada wanted to reduce its dependence on foreign sources of supply. Thus the Canadian government announced its decision to extend the Alberta-Sarnia (Ontario) pipeline to Montreal. Since the pipeline would have a flow of 250,000 barrels a day, and given that Canada's total oil production is peaking, the oil destined for the Montreal extension must come at the expense of exports to the United States.

In view of our previous discussion of Canada's dwindling energy resource base, the decision to cut back on exports is being accepted, in principle at least, in the United States as a necessary step in accordance with Canada's national interest. However, there is some question regarding the "need" to shut in, temporarily, the 250,000 barrels per day required to feed the Sarnia-Montreal line. Currently, eastern Canada imports over 800,000 barrels a day from OPEC producers, so that the pipeline extension will still leave eastern Canada vulnerable to any future possible disruptions in the flow of OPEC oil. Moreover, shutting in additional oil will extend Canada's self-sufficiency by a year or, perhaps, even less, and, at the same time, Canada will be inflicting greater hardship on U.S. refiners in the border areas. Thus, in the bilateral context, this decision does not go very far in serving Canadian national objectives, while at the same time, it has the potential of irritating the relationship further than is necessary.

Perhaps the greatest source of irritation concerns the fact that Canada did not adequately consult the United States when making its original decision to cut back on oil exports. This is particularly important in view of the fact that both countries face similar energy challenges in the longer term — e.g., greater dependence on imported oil and the need to develop high-cost, unconventional energy sources. By not allowing for sufficient prior consultation, Canada potentially risks having the United States exclude Canada in making its energy decisions in the next few years. The stakes are quite high when one considers that the development of Canada's frontier energy resources will depend to some extent on gaining access to the U.S. market in the late 1980s and 1990s. Fortunately, the Canadian government, recognizing the seriousness of this issue within the bilateral context, announced its intention of consulting with the United States before implementing any necessary cutbacks in natural gas.

Living with Natural Gas Shortages

As in the case of crude oil. Canadian exports of natural gas are essential to the economic well-being of selected gas users in the United States, notably in the midwest and west coast regions. However, since 1970 the National Energy Board has refused all applications for additional gas exports to the United States on the grounds that Canada does not have reserves surplus to its own requirements. In fact, some exports under existing contracts were cut because of production problems in the B.C. gas fields. Moreover, Canada intends, if necessary, to implement a generalized reduction in gas exports under existing licences, a decision that was based upon a National Energy Board report published last year that emphasized the inadequacy of current production in meeting domestic requirements.[12]

While the Canadian supply situations in oil and natural gas appear to be similar over the medium term, any decisions affecting gas exports are much more complex and potentially more sensitive in the bilateral context. Before turning to issues involved in natural gas trade, it should be emphasized that any gas export policy must recognize three important elements:

First, exports of Canadian oil are covered by thirty-day permits that must be renewed, while exports of Canadian gas are based on long-term contracts. Thus, aside from any possible legal considerations, Canada will be under strong pressure to fullfill what can be considered to be at least a moral obligation to meet natural gas export contracts.

Second, any export cutbacks would entail more difficult market adjustments in the United States than in the case of oil. There are no efficient alternatives to pipelines for natural gas, and the building of pipelines is very costly and is undertaken only on the basis of assurances of long-term supply availability.

---

[12] National Energy Board, *Canadian Natural Gas Supply and Requirements* (Ottawa, April, 1975), p. 84.

Third, future gas shortages in Canada and the United States tend to reflect the fact that natural gas has been priced below its true value as a source of energy for many years.

Pricing Exports

Taking the last point first, there is a general understanding between the two countries that the price of natural gas crossing the border must reflect full commodity value.[13] Where Canada and the United States differ, however, concerns the timing involved in moving to higher prices. In the spring of 1975, the National Energy Board recommended that the export price of gas should be increased from $1.00 per thousand cubic feet (mcf) to $1.60 per mcf effective August 1, 1975. The Canadian government, probably mindful of the suddenness of such a large increase, elected to apply this 60 percent increase in two stages — $1.40 per mcf as of August 1, 1975, and $1.60 as of November 1, 1975. It can be expected that the United States will press Canada not to move too quickly to full commodity value in order to ease the burden of adjustment in the U.S. market.

Domestically, Canada has embarked on a policy of moving the domestic price of natural gas to an appropriate competitive relationship with other fuels, especially oil, over the next two to four years.[14] At the time of writing (May, 1976), Canada's domestic oil price is lower than the U.S. price, and the use of commodity-value pricing for Canadian gas in the domestic and export markets has created, temporarily, a two-price system. The wholesale price into Toronto is $1.25 per mcf, and the border price is $1.60, both as of November 1, 1975[15] (although, unlike the case with oil, the difference between the export price and the domestic price is being channeled back to the producer). However, recent policy statements by the federal government strongly indicate that the Canadian domestic oil price will be moving closer to international levels within the next few years, meaning that the current difference between the domestic and export prices of gas will narrow with time.[16]

Sharing the Shortages

To many Americans, having to pay more for Canadian gas becomes secondary to a much more pressing issue — access to sup-

---

[13] Commodity value is a term used to describe the value of natural gas in relation to other available competitive fuels. Depending on the location, oil heating fuels, electricity, and even coal are used as reference points for pricing purposes. The National Energy Board advocates the use of a weighting system based on available alternative fuels in setting the Canadian export price, wherever possible.

[14] Energy, Mines and Resources Canada, op. cit., pp. 126-28.

[15] On May 19, 1976, the federal government announced that the domestic price of natural gas would increase to $1.40½ per mcf on July 1, 1976, and to $1.50½ per mcf on January 1, 1977. At the same time, it was announced that the export price would also increase, but no new price level was specified.

[16] Energy, Mines and Resources Canada, op. cit., pp. 126-28.

ply. The fear of natural gas shortages in both countries has increased substantially. In the United States, industry is worried about potential gas shortages and is actively seeking alternative sources of fuel. There is a threat that unemployment in certain areas would rise sharply if factories have to shut down for lack of natural gas. Earlier, the National Energy Board announced that Canada will also experience shortages in the next few years but the domestic supply situation in the short run has improved in recent months and shortages are not anticipated through 1977-78.

In dealing with Canada's potential gas shortages, the federal government is prepared to cut back natural gas exports and to reduce the rate of growth of natural gas use by Canadian industry and utilities. However, in this instance Ottawa's approach to the problem of export restrictions in the bilateral relationship is more conciliatory than it was with oil. The former Minister for Energy, Mines and Resources, Donald S. Macdonald, has stated that

> the government intends that reasonable Canadian requirements are met consistent with the wise use of this scarce natural resource, but that other demands are to be discouraged so as to enable our obligations to existing U.S. customers to be met to the greatest extent possible.[17]

Moreover, Canada intends to decide on both the timing and the amounts of the cutbacks after consultation with Washington.

While this approach does go a long way towards easing bilateral tensions in the energy field, there still remains an important question to resolve — how are the shortages to be shared?

The U.S. position in this matter of sharing has been that, on moral grounds at least, all shortages must be shared equally between the two countries. Actually, this demand was voiced in connection with the shortages in B.C. gas production, in which case the full burden of the shortages was borne by U.S. customers. As the B.C. situation indicates, there is a great reluctance on the part of many Canadians to share any shortages. Caught between domestic pressures and international obligations, the Canadian authorities now face a difficult decision, and one that will make neither domestic nor U.S. customers completely happy. Yet in view of the hardships that ensue from any reduction in gas supplies to U.S. users, Canada has a moral obligation to ease that hardship as much as it possibly can, even if it means imposing some shortages on the domestic market.

Finally, the issue of timing the export reductions is also of serious concern to the United States. It was emphasized earlier that the adjustment process in U.S. markets to a curtailment of Canadian gas export will be much more difficult than in the case of oil because

---

[17] "National Energy Board Report on Canadian Gas Demand, Supply and Deliverability," News Release (Ottawa: Department of Energy, Mines and Resources, July 15, 1975).

of the lack of alternative transportation modes to expensive, fixed pipelines. In this connection, Canada has little choice but to reduce the export flow of gas on a more gradual basis than it intends to do with oil.

Conclusions

One of the realties that currently shape Canada-U.S. relations is Canada's insistence that there be limits set on the degree of economic continentalism. This is nowhere as strikingly evident as in Canada's approach to bilateral energy matters. In a 1975 meeting with President Ford, Canada's then Energy Minister, Donald Macdonald, clearly rejected any "continentalist" solution to North America's energy problem; no longer can the United States expect unrestricted sales of Canada's energy resources. This position was taken in large measure because Canada will have such a substantial job developing sufficient supplies for its own needs over the next decade that it will not be in a position to undertake the development of special projects that would provide exports to the United States. In this respect, President Ford, responding to the Canadian position, recognized that Canada has to act in its own "enlightened self-interest" by taking steps to protect its future energy supplies.

Meanwhile, a rejection of the "continentalist" approach should not preclude the two countries from entering into joint projects that would greatly reduce the costs of pursuing independent energy policies. A recent statement by the Canadian-American Committee, *Keeping Options Open in Canada-U.S. Oil and Natural Gas Trade*, stressed that "numerous opportunities exist for cooperative action to achieve transportation efficiencies which would be in the national interest of both countries at whatever level of net exports of oil and natural gas may be decided upon by Canada."[18] The statement provides two important examples of the kind of cooperation that is needed:

● A formalized bilateral agreement on pipelines that would guarantee transmission rights. Such an agreement has recently been initialed by the two countries and, once formalized, should remove serious risks for the consuming nation and the pipeline owner regarding transit taxes, sudden price increases, or interruptions in the product flow.

● Energy-swapping arrangements that would increase the efficiency with which energy is transported to markets. In many cases, this can be done fairly readily; for example, some have advocated that the United States deliver Alaskan oil to British Columbia in exchange for an equivalent amount of Canadian oil to northern U.S. refineries.

---

[18] Montreal and Washington, 1975, p. 25.

In sum, in the short run the two countries are being forced to make difficult adjustments to rapidly changing demand and supply conditions, and these adjustments have generated bilateral tensions. However, in the long run both countries face similar energy challenges in having to contend with increasingly scarce and expensive energy, where opportunities will exist for a coordination of policies that would not necessarily compromise national policies and goals.

6

Concluding Comments

Many of the issues examined in this report arise from developments that extend far beyond the context of Canada-U.S. relations. Inflation, recession, and energy challenges are global in their scope and impact, and an effective resolution of the problems they have created must be sought through international means based on sound domestic policies. Transitions have been, and continue to be, made in response to important changes in the economic, political, and social environment facing the international community, but it would be premature to conclude that the adjustments in expectations and actions required to restore reasonable stability will be forthcoming. Inflationary pressures persist, unemployment remains unacceptably high, and long-term approaches to meeting energy needs are lacking.

The immediate future, however, is likely to be a distinct improvement over the recent past. Economic growth has begun to accelerate, paced by a solid recovery in the United States; inflation rates in almost all industrialized countries have improved considerably from a year ago; and world oil prices and supplies appear to have stabilized. Global recession has created, at a very high cost, a temporary "breathing space" within which effective policies for the future can be devised and implemented. Whether or not this time will be used wisely remains an open question, with the viability of existing economic and political systems potentially hanging in the balance.

Moving from the global to the bilateral, an improved economic outlook should contribute positively to several problem areas in Canada-U.S. relations. Canada's automotive trade deficit with the United States, for example, should be reduced significantly with a continuation of the kind of improved U.S. sales performance for North American vehicles registered in recent months. At a more general level, Canada has traditionally benefited from the demand for imports generated in an expansion phase of the U.S. business cycle. Even so, production costs in Canada have risen faster than in the United States for several years, and this situation creates the need for adjustments in coming months and years that will be difficult but essential if Canada is to meet its economic objectives and potential.

It would be shortsighted, however, to focus exclusively on the near-term economic aspects of the bilateral relationship. Certain major trends have become clearly visible in this relationship, and these trends predate the global economic disturbances of the past few years. These trends can be summarized by reviewing two themes that have recurred, at least implicitly, throughout this report.

The first theme is that both Canada and the United States are embarking upon new policy directions in response to a variety of domestic and international pressures and imperatives. In the case of the United States, new international policy directions have been necessitated by, and taken in response to, changes in that country's relative role and power in global economic and political relations. The impact of these new policy directions on Canada was not the primary consideration in the United States, but Canada has nevertheless been forced to take initiatives on its own as a defensive reaction.

But Canada's new policy initiatives go beyond strictly defensive responses. A clear trend has emerged in which Canada has asserted itself not only to reduce a perceived "vulnerability" to the United States but to carve out a more distinct Canadian "identity" in economic, cultural, and foreign affairs. These initiatives, which in a number of instances have appeared to outsiders to border on protectionism, have come as often from provincial governments as from the federal government. They have also risen largely from concerns that are judged important by a large number of Canadians and that have been recognized as such by the U.S. government. Still, the speed and scope of these initiatives threaten to create a "backlash" among an increasing number of U.S. citizens, and one is tempted to ask whether Canada has given sufficient attention to the distinction between what is politically desirable in the short run and what is economically necessary in the long run. At some point a danger will arise that, by placing the highest priority on too many objectives at one time, the capacity for bilateral cooperation will be exceeded. If the Canada-U.S. relationship is to remain "unique," this danger point must be avoided.

A second theme is that the momentum for positive, forward-looking bilateral agreements between Canada and the United States appears to be spent, at least for the present. Attention has been focused in both countries on explanations of why bilateral policy issues have emerged, but suggestions as to how to resolve these issues are now too often either lacking or put forward hesitantly and defensively. This situation may be the result of a concern that suggestions for cooperative approaches either will be misinterpreted as "continentalist" in Canada or will otherwise offend national sensitivities in either country.

The past several years have seen, at best, a holding action in the bilateral relationship. Over the next two years or so, Canada and the United States will face new pressures to determine whether a cooperative accommodation to changing domestic and international circumstances can be achieved. Areas where mutually advantageous accommodation might be reached are being clarified. To cite two examples: it is increasingly recognized that both countries face essentially similar energy challenges, and the possible economies from coordinated transportation facilities would make a contribution to meeting these challenges; and the key role of investment in generating non-inflationary growth is creating a new awareness of the potential costs of artificial barriers to investment flows across the border in both directions.

Commentators in Canada-U.S. relations seem to have a compulsion to make sweeping generalities about the state of the overall relationship as being either "good" or "bad" at a particular point in time. The conclusion to be drawn from this report is that broad generalizations of this sort are neither particularly informative nor appropriate. Difficult transitions, often leading to bilateral frictions, are a fact of the contemporary scene. The fundamental question is whether Canada and the United States will continue to perceive the advantages to their own self-interests in approaching these frictions in a spirit of cooperation in keeping with a relationship that is unique by circumstance, if not always by choice.

Co-Chairmen

ROBERT M. MacINTOSH
Executive Vice-President,
The Bank of Nova Scotia,
Toronto, Ontario

RICHARD J. SCHMEELK
Partner, Salomon Brothers,
New York, New York

Members

I. W. ABEL
President, United Steelworkers of America,
AFL-CIO, Pittsburgh, Pennsylvania

JOHN N. ABELL
Vice President and Director, Wood Gundy
Limited, Toronto, Ontario

R. L. ADAMS
Executive Vice President, Continental Oil
Company, Stamford, Connecticut

J. A. ARMSTRONG
President and Chief Executive Officer, Imperial Oil Limited, Toronto, Ontario

IAN A. BARCLAY
Chairman and Chief Executive Officer,
British Columbia Forest Products Limited,
Vancouver, British Columbia

MICHEL BELANGER
President, Provincial Bank of Canada,
Montreal, Quebec

ROY F. BENNETT
President and Chief Executive Officer, Ford
Motor Company of Canada, Limited, Oakville, Ontario

ROD J. BILODEAU
Chairman of the Board, Honeywell Limited,
Scarborough, Ontario

ROBERT BLAIR
President and Chief Executive Officer, Alberta Gas Trunk Line Company Limited,
Calgary, Alberta

BART H. BOSSIDY
Group Vice President — International Fibers, Celanese Corporation, New York, New
York

J. E. BRENT
Chairman of the Board, IBM Canada Ltd.,
Toronto, Ontario

PHILIP BRIGGS
Senior Vice President, Metropolitan Life Insurance Company, New York, New York

ARDEN BURBIDGE
Burbidge Farm, Park River, North Dakota

NICHOLAS J. CAMPBELL, JR.
Director and Senior Vice President, Exxon
Corporation, New York, New York

SHIRLEY CARR
Executive Vice-President, Canadian Labour
Congress, Ottawa, Ontario

W. R. CLERIHUE
Executive Vice-President, Staff and Administration, Celanese Corporation, New York,
New York

HON. JOHN V. CLYNE
MacMillan Bloedel Limited, Vancouver,
British Columbia

STANTON R. COOK
President, Tribune Company, Chicago, Illinois

THOMAS E. COVEL
Marion, Massachusetts

GEORGE B. CURRIE
Vancouver, British Columbia

RAYMOND L. DAVIS
International Trade Affairs Representative,
National Association of Wheat Growers, Potter, Nebraska

J. S. DEWAR
President, Union Carbide Canada Limited,
Toronto, Ontario

JOHN H. DICKEY
President, Nova Scotia Pulp Limited,
Halifax, Nova Scotia

JOHN S. DICKEY
President Emeritus and Bicentennial Professor of Public Affairs, Dartmouth College,
Hanover, New Hampshire

THOMAS W. diZEREGA
Vice President, Northwest Pipeline Corporation, Salt Lake City, Utah

WILLIAM DODGE
Ottawa, Ontario

A. D. DUNTON
Professor and Director, Institute of Canadian
Studies, Carleton University, Ottawa, Ontario

STEPHEN C. EYRE
Comptroller, First National City Bank, New
York, New York

A. J. FISHER
President, Fiberglas Canada Limited, Toronto, Ontario

CHARLES F. FOGARTY
Chairman and Chief Executive Officer,
Texasgulf Inc., New York, New York

ROBERT M. FOWLER
President, C. D. Howe Research Institute, Montreal, Quebec

JOHN F. GALLAGHER
Vice President, International Operations, Sears, Roebuck and Company, Chicago, Illinois

CARL J. GILBERT
Dover, Massachusetts

WAYNE E. GLENN
Vice Chairman, Continental Oil Company, Stamford, Connecticut

DONALD R. GRANGAARD
President, First Bank System, Inc., Minneapolis, Minnesota

PAT GREATHOUSE
Vice President, International Union, UAW, Detroit, Michigan

A. D. HAMILTON
President and Chief Executive Officer, Domtar Limited, Montreal, Quebec

JOHN A. HANNAH
Dansville, Michigan

ROBERT H. HANSEN
Group Vice-President, Avon Products, Inc., New York, New York

G. L. HARROLD
President, Alberta Wheat Pool, Calgary, Alberta

F. PEAVEY HEFFELFINGER
Director Emeritus, Peavey Company, Minneapolis, Minnesota

R. A. IRWIN
Chairman, Consolidated-Bathurst Limited, Montreal, Quebec

EDGAR F. KAISER, JR.
President and Chief Executive Officer, Kaiser Resources Ltd., Vancouver, British Columbia

JOSEPH D. KEENAN
International Secretary, International Brotherhood of Electrical Workers, AFL-CIO, Washington, D.C.

DONALD P. KELLY
President and Chief Operating Officer, Esmark, Inc., Chicago, Illinois

DAVID KIRK
Executive Secretary, The Canadian Federation of Agriculture, Ottawa, Ontario

LANE KIRKLAND
Secretary-Treasurer, AFL-CIO, Washington, D.C.

WILLIAM J. KUHFUSS
Mackinaw, Illinois

J. L. KUHN
President and General Manager, 3M Canada Limited, London, Ontario

HERBERT H. LANK
Director, Du Pont of Canada Limited, Montreal, Quebec

PAUL LEMAN
President, Alcan Aluminium Limited, Montreal, Quebec

EDMOND A. LEMIEUX
General Manager — Finance, Hydro-Quebec, Montreal, Quebec

FRANKLIN A. LINDSAY
Chairman, Itek Corporation, Lexington, Massachusetts

L. H. LORRAIN
President, Canadian Paperworkers Union, Montreal, Quebec

WILBER H. MACK
Chairman and Chief Executive Officer, American Natural Gas Company, Detroit, Michigan

M. W. MACKENZIE
Vice Chairman, Canron Limited, Montreal, Quebec

WILLIAM MAHONEY
National Director, United Steelworkers of America, AFL-CIO-CLC, Toronto, Ontario

JULIEN MAJOR
Executive Vice-President, Canadian Labour Congress, Ottawa, Ontario

PAUL M. MARSHALL
President, Canadian Hydrocarbons Ltd., Calgary, Alberta

FRANCIS L. MASON
Senior Vice President, The Chase Manhattan Bank, New York, New York

DENNIS McDERMOTT
UAW International Vice President and Director for Canada, International Union, UAW of America, Willowdale, Ontario

WILLIAM J. McDONOUGH
Executive Vice President, The First National Bank of Chicago, Chicago, Illinois

WILLIAM C. Y. McGREGOR
International Vice President, Brotherhood of Railway, Airline and Steamship Clerks, Montreal, Quebec

H. WALLACE MERRYMAN
Chairman and Chief Executive Officer, Avco Financial Services, Inc., Newport Beach, California

JOHN MILLER
President, National Planning Association, Washington, D.C.

COLMAN M. MOCKLER, JR.
Chairman and President, The Gillette Company, Boston, Massachusetts

DONALD R. MONTGOMERY
Secretary-Treasurer, Canadian Labour Congress, Ottawa, Ontario

JOSEPH MORRIS
President, Canadian Labour Congress, Ottawa, Ontario

RICHARD W. MUZZY
Vice President—International, Owens-Corning Fiberglas Corporation, Toledo, Ohio

THEODORE NELSON
Executive Vice President, Mobil Oil Corporation, New York, New York

THOMAS S. NICHOLS, SR.
Director, Olin Corporation, New York, New York

CARL E. NICKELS, JR.
Vice President, Finance and Administration, The Hanna Mining Company, Cleveland, Ohio

JOSEPH E. NOLAN
President and Trustee, Weyerhaeuser Company Foundation, Tacoma, Washington

HON. VICTOR deB. OLAND
Halifax, Nova Scotia

CHARLES PERRAULT
President, Perconsult Ltd., Montreal, Quebec

RICHARD H. PETERSON
Vice Chairman of the Board, Pacific Gas and Electric Company, San Francisco, California

BEN L. ROUSE
Vice-President — International Group, Burroughs Corporation, Detroit, Michigan

HENRY E. RUSSELL
President, Boston Safe Deposit and Trust Company, Boston, Massachusetts

THOMAS W. RUSSELL, JR.
Senior Vice President, Haley Associates, Inc., New York, New York

A. E. SAFARIAN
Dean, School of Graduate Studies, University of Toronto, Toronto, Ontario

W. B. SAUNDERS
Group Vice President, Cargill, Incorporated, Minneapolis, Minnesota

HON. ADOLPH W. SCHMIDT
Ligonier, Pennsylvania

A. R. SLOAN
President and General Manager, Continental Can International, Stamford, Connecticut

EDSON W. SPENCER
President and Chief Executive Officer, Honeywell Inc., Minneapolis, Minnesota

W. A. STRAUSS
Chairman and President, Northern Natural Gas Company, Omaha, Nebraska

ROBERT D. STUART, JR.
President, The Quaker Oats Company, Chicago, Illinois

A. McC. SUTHERLAND
Senior Vice President, The International Nickel Company of Canada, Limited, Toronto, Ontario

DWIGHT D. TAYLOR
Senior Vice President, Crown Zellerbach Corporation, San Francisco, California

ROBERT B. TAYLOR
Chairman, Ontario Hydro, Toronto, Ontario

WILLIAM I. M. TURNER, JR.
President and Chief Executive Officer, Consolidated-Bathurst Limited, Montreal, Quebec

W. O. TWAITS
Toronto, Ontario

MELVIN J. WERNER
Vice President, Farmers Union Grain Terminal Association, Saint Paul, Minnesota

JOHN R. WHITE
New York, New York

HENRY S. WINGATE
Formerly Chairman and Chief Officer, The International Nickel Company of Canada, Ltd., New York, New York

WILLIAM W. WINPISINGER
General Vice President, International Association of Machinists and Aerospace Workers, Washington, D.C.

THOMAS WINSHIP
Editor, *Boston Globe*, Boston, Massachusetts

FRANCIS G. WINSPEAR
Edmonton, Alberta

D. MICHAEL WINTON
Chairman, Pas Lumber Company Limited, Minneapolis, Minnesota

GEORGE W. WOODS
President, TransCanada Pipelines, Toronto, Ontario

WILLIAM S. WOODSIDE
President, American Can Company, Greenwich, Connecticut

ADAM H. ZIMMERMAN
Executive Vice President, Noranda Mines Limited, Toronto, Ontario

Honorary Members

EDWARD F. BLETTNER
Honorary Director, The First National Bank of Chicago, Chicago, Illinois

HON. N. A. M. MacKENZIE
Vancouver, British Columbia

HAROLD SWEATT
Honorary Chairman of the Board, Honeywell Inc., Minneapolis, Minnesota

DAVID J. WINTON
Minneapolis, Minnesota

SELECTED PUBLICATIONS
OF THE CANADIAN-AMERICAN COMMITTEE*

Commercial Relations

CAC-42 *A Time of Difficult Transitions: Canada-U.S. Relations in 1976*, a Staff Report. 1976 ($2.00)

CAC-40 *Industrial Incentive Policies and Programs in the Canadian-American Context*, by John Volpe. 1976 ($2.50)

CAC-38 *A Balance of Payments Handbook*, by Caroline Pestieau. 1974 ($2.00)

CAC-32 *Toward a More Realistic Appraisal of the Automotive Agreement*, a Statement by the Committee. 1970 ($1.00)

CAC-31 *The Canada-U.S. Automotive Agreement: An Evaluation*, by Carl E. Beigie. 1970 ($3.00)

CAC-25 *A New Trade Strategy for Canada and the United States*, a Statement by the Committee. 1966 ($1.00)

CAC-23 *A Possible Plan for a Canada-U.S. Free Trade Area*, a Staff Report. 1965 ($1.50)

CAC-21 *A Canada-U.S. Free Trade Arrangement: Survey of Possible Characteristics*, by Sperry Lea. 1963 ($2.00)

Energy and Other Resources

CAC-41 *Coal and Canada-U.S. Energy Relations*, by Richard L. Gordon. 1976 ($3.00)

CAC-39 *Keeping Options Open in Canada-U.S. Oil and Natural Gas Trade*, a Statement by the Committee. 1975 ($1.00)

CAC-37 *Canada, the United States, and the Third Law of the Sea Conference*, by R. M. Logan. 1974 ($3.00)

CAC-36 *Energy from the Arctic: Facts and Issues*, by Judith Maxwell. 1973 ($4.00)

Investment

CAC-33 *Canada's Experience with Fixed and Flexible Exchange Rates in a North-American Capital Market*, by Robert M. Dunn, Jr. 1971 ($2.00)

CAC-29 *The Performance of Foreign-Owned Firms in Canada*, by A. E. Safarian. 1969 ($2.00)

CAC-24 *Capital Flows Between Canada and the United States*, by Irving Brecher. 1965 ($2.00)

---

* These and other Committee publications may be ordered from the Committee's offices at 2064 Sun Life Building, Montreal, Quebec H3B 2X7, and at 1606 New Hampshire Avenue, N.W., Washington, D. C. 20009. Quantity discounts are given. A descriptive flyer of these publications is also available.